"*Get Your Teenager Talking* is the perfect tool for connecting with today's teenagers, a generation that often has a difficult time opening up to adults."

—Dr. Kevin Leman, author of *Have a New Teenager by Friday*

"As a parent, this is such a practical tool—it's an arsenal for those of us who need some prompters to get our kids talking in more than grunts and one-word answers. Jonathan McKee serves parents with insightful tips on how to stimulate conversation to provoke meaningful dialogue. Parents, this is the stuff that matters!"

—Doug Fields, executive director of HomeWord
Youth & Family at Azusa Pacific University;
co-founder of downloadyouthministry.com

"If your teenager answers you with one-word replies, shrugs, or the occasional eye roll accompanied with a sigh, buy this book! You'll be on your way—quickly—to fun, meaningful conversations."

—Vicki Hitzges, international motivational speaker/author

"Calling this book practical is an almost-ridiculous understatement: it's a bounty of creative starters for deep conversations between teenagers and parents! There are plenty of helpful, theoretical parenting books on the market; but Jonathan's book isn't merely one to think about, it's a gift to be used."

—Mark Oestreicher, partner in The Youth Cartel

"Take note, parenting-book authors: this is how to write for today's parents. Rather than giving us another lecture on how important it is to talk with our kids (big-time guilt trip), how about giving us some great ideas (180 or so) for starting conversations with them in a fun and natural way (big-time success!). Well played, Jon McKee!"

—Wayne Rice, pastor to generations at College Avenue Baptist
Church (San Diego, CA); co-founder of Youth Specialties

"We as parents of teens run out of things to say and ask our kids. Fear no more! If you want fun, clever, and witty ways to engage your adolescent, pick up Jonathan McKee's *Get Your Teenager Talking* and let the conversations begin."

—Dr. David Olshine, professor and director
of Youth Ministry, Family and Culture
at Columbia International University (Columbia, SC)

"Few people understand the teenage world like Jonathan McKee. This book is one of the most helpful and practical tools I have ever seen to get teenagers talking with their parents about important topics. Authorities tell us that when parents and teens have meaningful, value-centered conversations in the home, teens will stay more engaged with their family, faith, and values. This is a most valuable resource for parents and those who work with kids."

—Jim Burns, PhD, author of *Teenology: The Art of Raising Great Teenagers* and *Confident Parenting*

GET YOUR
TEENAGER
TALKING

GET YOUR TEENAGER TALKING

EVERYTHING YOU NEED TO
SPARK MEANINGFUL CONVERSATIONS

JONATHAN McKEE

BETHANY HOUSE PUBLISHERS

a division of Baker Publishing Group
Minneapolis, Minnesota

Published by Bethany House Publishers
11400 Hampshire Avenue South
Bloomington, Minnesota 55438
www.bethanyhouse.com

Bethany House Publishers is a division of
Baker Publishing Group, Grand Rapids, Michigan

Printed in the United States of America

Library of Congress Cataloging-in-Publication Data
McKee, Jonathan R. (Jonathan Ray).
    Get your teenager talking : everything you need to spark meaningful conversations / Jonathan McKee.
        pages cm
    Includes bibliographical references and index.
    Summary: "Offering discussion starters, follow-up questions, and interpretations of common responses, these 180 creative ways to get conversations going will help parents and youth workers connect with teens"—Provided by publisher.
    ISBN 978-0-7642-1185-0 (pbk. : alk. paper)
    1. Parent and teenager. 2. Interpersonal communication. 3. Teenagers.
I. Title.
    HQ799.15.M327 2014
    305'.235—dc23   2013047293

Cover design by LOOK Design Studio

Author is represented by WordServe Literary Group

14 15 16 17 18 19 20   7 6 5 4 3 2 1

*To all the parents out there
who desperately would love to
connect with their kids.
'Cause it ain't easy.*

Thanks to my three,
Alec, Alyssa, and Ashley,
*who bear with me
when I try.*

Contents

5 Tips to Get Your Teenager Talking

Is it just me, or do you sometimes struggle getting teenagers to open up and just talk?

I have this issue with my own teenagers. Conversations can drift toward the mundane.

"How was school?"

"Fine."

"Soccer practice?"

"Same as always."

"Anything interesting happen today?"

"Nope."

"Nice talking with you!"

When I was a youth worker I faced the same frustrations talking with teenagers the first time.

"What's your name?"

"Chris."

"What school do you go to?"

"Centerville High."

"Play any sports?"

"Nope."

(awkward pause)

"Have you ever accidently killed a squirrel?"

"Huh?"

"Never mind."

Let's face it. Teenagers have a PhD in one-word answers . . . if we don't ask the right questions.

That's the key—asking questions. When you ask questions, it shows you care.

Jesus is someone who constantly noticed people and took time to ask them questions. He paid attention to outcasts and even notorious sinners. In turn, they followed him and many put their trust in him. Perhaps we should follow his example of taking the time to notice our kids and ask well-placed questions.

Often, today's adults don't take any interest in teenagers. They're ignoring some of the best parenting advice ever written. Several thousand years ago, Moses instructed his people to love the Lord their God with all their heart, soul, and strength (Deuteronomy 6:5), but he didn't stop there. He told them to impress these commandments on their children as they sit at home, as they walk along the road, when they lie down, and when they get up (v. 7).

That's quite a mandate if you think about it: morning, noon, and night, having conversations while you are sitting and walking. Moses paints a clear picture of a parent who is giving regular instruction as they go through life together.

But that still leaves many of us wondering, What does this look like in my home today? In other words: How can I actually get my teenager to talk to me?

Here are 5 tips that help
me get teenagers talking:

1 ### Don't ask yes or no questions.

If you ask a *yes* or *no* question, you know you're going to get a one-word answer.

If you ask a teenager, "Was school fun today?" Chances are, you're going to hear the word "No."

Conversation over.

What good is that? We need to start thinking proactively and come up with questions that require more than one-word responses. And that leads me to my second tip . . .

2 *Don't ask dull questions.*

Parents always complain to me that they can't get their kids to talk with them, but often they don't put any time into formulating their questions. If all we ask our kids is "How was your day?" and it never gets any response, why do we keep asking it?

My daughter Alyssa told it to me straight one day:

"Dad, stop asking me how school is day after day. School's always the same. It sucks, it's boring, and it seems like a waste of time. I could cram all seven hours of what they teach me into about ninety minutes. So stop asking me the same question. You're just gonna get the same answer."

Wow. I guess I should give her credit for being honest!

So instead of asking "How was school?" how about asking something like this:

"If you could ditch all your classes tomorrow except one, which class would you choose to actually attend? Why?"

A question like this gives you insight into what subjects they like, what kind of adults they respect, plus it provides them with a fun element—picturing a world where they choose classes and ditch others!

"I'd probably go to English. Mr. Alves is pretty cool, and we're reading *Huck Finn* right now, which is actually pretty good."

If we're willing to put a little more thought into our questions, we might get a little more from their responses. But unexpected questions don't always come easy, that's why you always need to . . .

3 *Think ahead.*

If you struggle getting your teenager to talk, don't try to think of something on the fly. Plan ahead.

Parents, don't wait until you're sitting at the dinner table to try to think of something to say. Think ahead. Use some resources if you have to. You're holding a great one in your hand. But this book isn't the only source that will help you spark meaningful conversations, which brings me to my next tip . . .

4 *Use controversy.*

If you want to talk to your kid about parental guidelines, for instance, you could approach it one of two ways. You could say, "Hey, wanna talk about parental guidelines?" But be careful if he has fruit or muffins in his hands when you ask this, he is liable to throw them at you. Honestly, what kid is going to respond to that kind of proposal?

Instead, try this: "Hey, did you see the YouTube video where the redneck dad got so sick of his daughter's disrespectful antics on Facebook that he pulled out his .45 and blew holes in her laptop?"

I tried that with my daughters and they both laughed, demanding to see the video immediately. Afterward, I asked, "So do you think the dad was unfair?" It resulted in a forty-five-minute discussion about parental guidelines.

Want to talk with your daughter about the pressures she's going to face at school dances? Again, you could try your luck asking her to sit down on the couch so you can discuss it, or you could rent the remake of *Footloose*, watch it together, and then ask some well-placed questions about what you saw.

I find that kids can be provoked by controversy. Share a story from the newspaper about a current event and simply ask, "Were they right?"

I remember reading about a local kid who was kicked out of a private school. He had signed a contract, committing to a strict dress code that included hair cut over the ears for boys. Over the summer the boy didn't cut his hair and returned to school, violating the dress code. After several warnings, the school finally kicked the boy out of school. The family called the press and made a big fuss.

I brought up the boy's story with my kids and asked, "Was he right?"

It was fun to hear the debate around my kitchen table. Some were arguing about hair length and legalism, but others simply argued, "He signed a contract!"

All I did was share a story and ask one three-word question: "Was he right?" The result? Heated debate.

Pop culture offers plenty of creative discussion starters through songs, movies, and current events. Just go to the front page of my website TheSource4Parents.com and you'll find a myriad of youth culture studies and articles. I constantly am reading and linking articles about technology, celebrities, entertainment media, drugs, and alcohol . . . all can be used as discussion springboards to get your teenager talking.

5   *Use your eyes and ears before your mouth.*

I truly saved my best tip for last. Simply put: *notice.*

Notice their interests. When our teenagers are quiet, it's not because they don't have anything to say. Far from it. Most teenagers will talk your ear off . . . if you can stir them to express themselves about things they're passionate about. The biggest reason we can't get our kids to talk is because we're asking them the wrong questions and we're not noticing opportunities for conversation.

Use your ears to notice what songs or musical artist they keep talking about. If you hear your daughter is constantly talking about how much she loves Adam Levine, ask her about him:

"What's your favorite Maroon 5 song?"
"What do you think of their new album?"
"While we're in the car together, play me some Adam Levine."

Similarly, use your eyes to notice what shirts your teenager likes—it will tell you a lot. If he wants to buy vintage *Star Wars* T-shirts, that could probably lead to him talking

15

about nerdy topics for hours. If he wants a Seattle Seahawks jersey . . . *he really needs Jesus!*

In the same way, if you hear a teenager get intrigued by something like the latest iPhone, chances are you won't have to say much to get her talking about it. Notice what teenagers are excited about, ask them about it, and then you won't have to do much talking at all. You might even wish you never got them started!

Remember, our teenagers really want to be heard. Sadly, they often are ignored by adults. So sometimes they just need to test the waters and see that we're actually willing to listen.

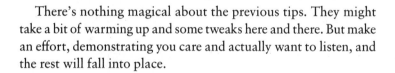

There's nothing magical about the previous tips. They might take a bit of warming up and some tweaks here and there. But make an effort, demonstrating you care and actually want to listen, and the rest will fall into place.

180

CONVERSATION
SPRINGBOARDS

How to Use This Book

I think you'll find this book easy to use. Each page contains keys specifically crafted to open the doors of dialogue with young people. Occasionally these conversation starters will lead to talk about values, and this is a great opportunity to draw from the Bible, a source of amazing wisdom. But let these moments flow naturally.

Feel free to work your way through the conversation springboards in order. Another option is to flip through the book and see what question, story, or quote catches your attention or somehow seems best for a particular time or situation. Even so, if you do hope to steer a conversation toward a certain topic, such as school, friends, or faith, you'll find an index in the back. The questions are written from a parent's perspective, but the exact wording can be easily adjusted for youth leaders, teachers, and everyone else who wants to help a teen feel noticed and heard.

Just remember, there's no need to force anything.

That's the beauty of asking questions. Questions create dialogue . . . *not a monologue*. Kids don't want to hear our monologue.

Now let's dive into some questions that will get your teenager talking!

Conversation SPRINGBOARD 1

If you could text anyone in the world right now, and he or she would actually text you back, who would you text?

Follow-Up Questions

- What would you ask that person?
- What do you think they'd probably reply?
- How would that make you feel?
- Why would you choose that person?

Insight Into the Question

These questions not only give you insight into your kid's heroes or crushes, they provide a peek into his feelings about this person.

Quick Additions

- If you could only text one person for the next year—someone you already text regularly—who would you choose?
- Why that person?
- Who would you really miss texting during that year?

Conversation SPRINGBOARD 2

If you could eliminate one evil in the world, what would you destroy, and why?

Follow-Up Questions

- Describe this new world.
- How would this change your typical day?
- In reality, since we don't have the power to eliminate evil, what is something people *could* do that would help battle this evil?
- What part could you play in this?

Insight Into the Question

This question gets young people thinking about real-world problems and possible solutions.

Quick Additions

- What are some common evils you see every day?
- What are some common good things you see people do?
- Who is someone you know or observe who inspires others to do good?
- How could you inspire others?

Conversation SPRINGBOARD 3

A nationwide survey asked people about the appropriate use of cell phones in social settings such as mealtimes, meetings, and in classrooms. The answers varied considerably by the respondent's age. The younger the person, the more they perceived texting as permissible in social settings. For example, 50 percent of younger people—ages eighteen to twenty-nine—considered texting during a meal permissible, compared with only 15 percent of those age thirty and older. Similarly, 33 percent of the younger people considered texting during a meeting appropriate, compared with 17 percent of those age thirty and older.[1]

Why do you think younger people find it more appropriate to text during meals and meetings?

Follow-Up Questions

- Do you think it's appropriate to text during a meal? Explain.
- Why do you think the majority of people thirty and older find this rude?
- When a young person is dining or meeting with someone older, how much should the younger person consider the older person's sense of etiquette?
- How much should the older person consider the younger person's sense of etiquette?

Insight Into the Question

This question stimulates young people to think about their manners and how others perceive them.

Quick Additions

- What are some other habits that young people tolerate but older people don't?
- Why do you think this is?
- Who needs to change? Explain.

Conversation **SPRINGBOARD 4**

The word *swagger* is used in songs, by celebrities, and by everyday people. What does "swag" or "swagger" mean to you?

Follow-Up Questions

The dictionary defines *swagger* as a verb, meaning "strut around" or "brag." It also can be defined as an arrogant walk.

- Can swagger be a good thing? Explain.
- Do you have a swag? If so, what does it communicate to others?
- Why do you think musicians/rappers refer to their swagger as if it's a positive thing?
- How do you think a person should "carry" herself?

Insight Into the Question

This question uses a popular term from pop culture to provoke discussion about pride, arrogance, and perhaps even self-esteem.

Quick Additions

- Do you think either of us (your parents) have or ever had any swag? Why or why not?
- If we don't have it, could we get it? How? (Note: these last two are meant to be light, humorous questions.)

Conversation SPRINGBOARD 5

Helen Keller once said, "Character cannot be developed in ease and quiet. Only through experience of trial and suffering can the soul be strengthened, ambition inspired, and success achieved."

Follow-Up Questions

- Why do you think she said this?
- What examples have you seen of someone growing and becoming stronger through a really tough situation?
- If you could somehow choose a difficult path that you know would help you develop character, what would you choose?

Insight Into the Question

Keller's quote reveals great wisdom. Young people today probably see in their own lives evidence of what she observed. This quote and these questions might help them connect those dots on their own.

Quick Additions

- Would you rather have a life with little pain and suffering, and only achieve mediocrity, or would you rather suffer and experience some very hard times, which cause you to grow and achieve great success? Explain.
- Give an example of someone undergoing suffering for the good of someone else.

Read the following Scripture:

For Christ also suffered once for sins, the righteous for the unrighteous, to bring you to God. He was put to death in the body but made alive in the Spirit.

1 Peter 3:18

- How far was Jesus willing to suffer to save us?
- Was it worth it? Explain.

Conversation SPRINGBOARD 6

Totally true: Not long ago a book was published titled *What Every Man Thinks About Apart from Sex.* All two hundred pages are completely blank. The book soared through the bestseller charts and became a craze on college campuses, where students used the blank pages to take notes.[2]

Why do you think the book was so successful?

Follow-Up Questions

- Do you think the book's premise is true? Why or why not?
- What do you think most of your guy friends think about most of the time?
- Why do you think that God made sex such a huge desire for men?

Insight Into the Question

Although some parents might feel hesitant to engage in this kind of conversation with their kids, dialogue like this is healthy. We need to consistently talk openly and candidly with our kids about sex—not explicitly or awkwardly, but honestly and tactfully. These nonconfrontational questions touch on the subject without going into great detail and show kids that their parents are safe to talk with about sex and relationships.

Quick Additions

- If "sex" is the topic that consumes the thinking of males, what consumes the thinking of females?
- Where do you see this day to day?
- If a book with blank pages was specifically written about you, what huge desire seems to control most of your thinking right now?

Conversation SPRINGBOARD 7

If you could get stuck in an elevator for eight hours with anyone in the world, who would you want to get stuck with?

Follow-Up Questions

- Why this person over any of the other people you hang out with day to day?

- What would you want to talk about with this person?
- Who is someone you know right now who you could maybe talk with about this same subject?

Insight Into the Question

This question gives you an idea of who is important to your kid. Hopefully, the follow-up questions will prompt him to evaluate his manner of conversation with certain people.

Quick Additions

- If you could add anyone else to the elevator, would you?
- Who would you add?
- What subject of conversation would you hope to avoid?
- Who would you not want in that elevator?

Conversation SPRINGBOARD 8

If I promised not to get upset, would you tell me if there's something I do that irritates you? What is it?

Follow-Up Questions

- If you could give me one piece of advice about this, what would you tell me?
- Do you think this thing drives others crazy too, or just you? Why?
- Do you think I should change my behavior?
- What is something you could do that might improve the situation?

Insight Into the Question

Only ask this question if you're truly ready to hear the answer and not overreact or argue. This is a great opportunity to listen to your teenager's perspective and, at the same time, give her a chance to think about how she can influence the situation good or bad.

Quick Additions

- What is something you do that might irritate someone in this family?
- Do you think it irritates other people too?
- Do you think it would be a good idea to change your behavior?
- What would it take to do that?
- Can I help?

Conversation SPRINGBOARD 9

Tell me something about the shirt you're wearing right now.

Follow-Up Questions

- Why did you choose this shirt today?
- What is your favorite shirt or outfit to wear, and why?
- Describe a shirt or other article of clothing you saw someone wearing recently that you liked.

Insight Into the Question

The clothes young people wear today tell us a lot about them. Those who are into fashion have lots of reasoning behind why they choose certain outfits. Even those who don't care about their clothing still have opinions, especially about what they would not wear!

Quick Additions

- Describe a clothing style that you do not like. Why not?
- If you were given a gift certificate for just one clothing store, enough to buy an entire wardrobe, what store would you choose . . . and why?
- Describe some items you would buy.
- Is there pressure in your social circles to dress a certain way? Explain.
- What would happen if you resisted those pressures?

Conversation SPRINGBOARD 10

What song is your go-to song you listen to whenever you are feeling sad?

Follow-Up Questions

- How does this song make you feel?
- What is it about this song that makes you feel this way?
- Do any specific lyrics resonate with you?

Insight Into the Question

This question uses the subject of music to get young people to talk about their feelings. (If your kid isn't a fan of music, feel free to skip this one.) Most young people spend several hours listening to music each day and identify with many songs and artists. Parents can learn a lot about their kids by tuning in to their musical tastes.

Quick Additions

- If this song were in a playlist, what would you name the playlist?
- What other songs would be in that playlist?
- Do you usually feel better, or worse, after listening to this playlist? Why?

Conversation SPRINGBOARD 11

What makes someone popular at your school?

Follow-Up Questions

- Do you have any of these qualities?
- If you could have one quality or characteristic that made you feel more accepted by others, what would you want?
- How long do external qualities (such as looks, athletic ability, etc.) last?
- How long do our internal qualities (character, kindness, compassion) last?

Insight Into the Question

This discussion gets kids thinking about the characteristics they are pursuing.

Quick Additions

Jesus asked, "What good is it to gain the whole world, and yet lose your soul?" (paraphrase of Luke 9:25).

- How do you see people trying to "gain the whole world"?
- What do you think Jesus meant by "lose your soul"?

- Why would someone cling on to temporary thrills and achievements, knowing they might have eternal consequences?
- What temporary thrills and achievements distract you at times?
- How can I help you stay focused on the truth? (Hebrews 12:1–2: "Let us throw off everything that hinders and the sin that so easily entangles. And let us run with perseverance the race marked out for us, fixing our eyes on Jesus, the pioneer and perfecter of faith.")

Conversation SPRINGBOARD 12

Novelist Jane Smiley describes marriage this way:

You know what getting married is? It's agreeing to taking this person who right now is at the top of his form, full of hopes and ideas, feeling good, looking good, wildly interested in you because you're the same way, and sticking by him while he slowly disintegrates. And he does the same for you. You're his responsibility now and he's yours. If no one else will take care of him, you will. If everyone else rejects you, he won't. What do you think love is? Going to bed all the time?

What is she trying to communicate?

Follow-Up Questions

- How does she describe two people when they are deciding to get married?
- Why do you think she uses the word "disintegrates" for what happens after marriage?
- Is this true? Explain.

Insight Into the Question

This question gets young people thinking about the realities of the marriage commitment.

Quick Additions

- Why do you think she describes love as sticking by each other and not rejecting one another, year after year, even when others do?
- How does this compare to the media's portrayal of love: "going to bed all the time"?
- What qualities should a young person look for in a spouse?
- What specific qualities are you going to look for?

Conversation SPRINGBOARD 13

What is your favorite phone app?

Follow-Up Questions

- What's so great about this app?
- How much time do you think you spend on this app each day?
- Is this too much? Explain.

Insight Into the Question

This question provides insight into young people's mobile device habits.

Quick Additions

- What other apps do you enjoy?
- What's an app you know I'd enjoy?
- What's an app you know I'd probably not like?

- What's an app you like, but you'd be scared to tell me you like it?

Conversation SPRINGBOARD 14

What was the best day of your life? Describe it.

Follow-Up Questions

- Why was this day so special?
- Have any other days been close to this day? Explain.
- What could happen in the future that would rank high with your best day?

Insight Into the Question

This reflective question prompts kids to reflect on good memories, and gives you insight as to what is special to them.

Quick Additions

- What was your worst day? Describe it.
- What made this day so bad?
- How did you get through it?
- How did this day change you?

Conversation SPRINGBOARD 15

Describe the top five qualities you want your future spouse to have.

Follow-Up Questions

- Which of these is the most important to you?

- Are any of these qualities negotiable?
- Is it important to date people with these qualities?

Insight Into the Question

This question gets young people thinking about the type of person they want to look for in a spouse.

Quick Additions

- Do you have any of these qualities? Which ones?

Read the following Scripture passage:

Love is patient, love is kind. It does not envy, it does not boast, it is not proud. It does not dishonor others, it is not self-seeking, it is not easily angered, it keeps no record of wrongs.

1 Corinthians 13:4–5

- If you could add one of these qualities to your list of five above, which would you add?
- Which of these qualities do you wish you had, but don't?
- Is that something you can work on? How?
- How can I help?

Conversation **SPRINGBOARD 16**

What possession do you treasure the most?

Follow-Up Questions

- Why is this so special to you?
- Is it replaceable? Why or why not?
- What would you do if it were lost or broken?
- Is your love for this item healthy? Explain why or why not.

Insight Into the Question

This question reveals what possessions your kid values, but perhaps also what motivates her.

Quick Additions

- Five years ago, what possession did you treasure the most?
- In five years, what do you think you'll treasure the most? Explain.
- In twenty years will it be something different? Why?

Conversation SPRINGBOARD 17

If you could have any occupation in the world, what would you want to do, and why?

Follow-Up Questions

- How does salary influence this decision?
- Where would you want to do this job, and why?
- Describe what you think your daily duties would look like.

Insight Into the Question

This question gets young people to use their imagination, consider careers, and evaluate the possibilities of pursuing their dreams.

Quick Additions

- What would it take to make this dream job a reality?
- What would you have to start doing to make this happen?
- To get this job, what actions might you have to avoid?

Conversation **SPRINGBOARD 18**

Warning: This conversation springboard deals with a mature subject matter: alcohol drinking and sexual assault. Personally, I believe it's essential for parents to have these conversations with their teenagers, but you should review these questions first and use your discretion.

The Center of Alcohol Studies at Rutgers University followed hundreds of young women from their senior year in high school through their freshman year of college. Two alarming discoveries were made:

- Of girls who had never drunk heavily in high school (if at all), nearly half admitted to binge drinking at least once by the end of their first college semester.
- Of all girls whose biggest binge had included four to six drinks in one sitting, one-fourth said they'd been sexually victimized in the fall semester. That included anything from unwanted sexual contact to rape. And the more alcohol those binges involved, the greater the likelihood of sexual assault. Of women who had consumed ten or more drinks in a sitting since starting college, 59 percent were sexually victimized by the end of their first semester.[3]

Why do you think half of girls who barely drank at high school, if at all, try drinking heavily once they get to college?

Follow-Up Questions

- What were some of the consequences the study uncovered?
- Why do you think heavy drinkers are more likely to experience sexual assault or unwanted sexual contact?
- Do you think most of these young women foresaw these consequences? Why or why not?
- How can high school and college students, particularly girls, be more responsible?

Insight Into the Question

This research and discussion unveils the harsh realities of binge drinking and its probable consequences.

Quick Additions

- How often do TV shows, movies, and songs mention drinking? (The answer is, a lot.)
- How often do these entertainment sources show consequences of binge drinking, such as rape, sexual assault, or unwanted sexual contact? (The answer is, seldom.)
- Why do you think entertainment media choose to ignore this reality?

Conversation SPRINGBOARD 19

When you were little, what did you want to be when you grew up?

Follow-Up Questions

- How has this changed as you've gotten older?
- What influences in your life have swayed your thinking on this?
- If you were to choose a career today that you'd have to keep the rest of your life, what would you choose, and why?

Insight Into the Question

This question helps young people think through possible careers and what is important when choosing one.

Quick Additions

- What is a job you never want, and why?

- If you could do that job and make an enormous salary, would you reconsider?
- Explain which is more important: enjoying your job, or money?

Conversation SPRINGBOARD 20

What is your favorite room in the house, and why?

Follow-Up Questions

- What do you like to do in there?
- What is a good memory you have of the room?
- Who do you like hanging out with in that room?

Insight Into the Question

This question gives you an insight into where your kid feels comfortable and likes to hang out, and also reveals what's important to her.

Quick Additions

- If you could make any upgrades to that room, what would you do, and why?
- What would you make sure to keep the same, and why?

Conversation SPRINGBOARD 21

Who is someone you could talk to about anything . . . even an embarrassing secret?

Follow-Up Questions

- How would this person respond if you told him or her something embarrassing?
- How would this person help you?

The Bible actually encourages us to share our struggles and sins with each other:

> Therefore confess your sins to each other and pray for each other so that you may be healed. The prayer of a righteous person is powerful and effective.
>
> James 5:16

- According to this verse, why should we confess our sins to each other and pray for each other?
- How do you think this heals us?

Insight Into the Question

This question helps kids think about with whom they can open up and be real. This could be the foundation of an accountability relationship.

Quick Additions

- What are some benefits of having someone who knows you this well?
- How could this person help you with struggles you have?

Conversation SPRINGBOARD 22

A recent survey of college students revealed their feelings about their gadgets. They were asked to select which piece of technology would most negatively impact their lives if it were lost. The number-one answer was their laptop. Second place was their phone. Third . . . *their car*.[4]

Why do you think most young people would be more upset if they lost their laptop or phone than their car?

Follow-Up Questions

- What do you think this survey would have discovered if it was done at your school—what would the number-one answer be?
- Why do you think most people value this?
- What piece of technology (car, TV, phone, Xbox, etc.) would you be the most upset to lose?
- Why would you miss this item the most?

Insight Into the Question

This question gives you a glimpse into your kid's world of technology.

Quick Additions

- What is your favorite activity with this gadget?
- Do you think you spend too much time with this gadget? Explain.
- What gadget do you think I'd miss the most?
- Do you think I spend too much time with this gadget? Explain.

Conversation SPRINGBOARD 23

If you could pick any state to live in in the United States, where would you want to live, and why?

Follow-Up Questions

- Which city would you live in?
- What is the weather like there?
- How does climate affect your decision to live in this location?
- What activities that you enjoy can you do in this state?

Insight Into the Question

This is simply a fun question to learn more about your kid's interests geographically.

Quick Additions

- If a future job would pay to move you to any state and work there, but your preferred state wasn't available, which state would you choose instead?
- Why this state?
- Why is your first choice better?
- Is there anything about the second state that is better than the first?

Conversation SPRINGBOARD 24

What is something in our house that you should probably get rid of, but haven't?

Follow-Up Questions

- What is it that people enjoy about this thing?
- What do you like about it?
- What harm does it do?
- Why do people keep it?
- Why is it still in our house?

Insight Into the Question

This question dives right into the distractions in our lives and the steps it might take to get rid of them.

Quick Additions

- Why is it hard to get rid of things like this?
- What would it take to get rid of it this week?
- How can I help?

Conversation SPRINGBOARD 25

If you could relive one day of your life, but this time, do something differently, what would you do?

Follow-Up Questions

- How would your life be different now?
- What were some of the consequences, good or bad, from the decisions you made that day the first time around?
- What have you learned from this experience?

Insight Into the Question

This question can open insight into some major life decisions your teenager regrets, and help him think through how he would handle similar decisions in the future.

Quick Additions

- If reliving the day meant forgetting this wisdom you have gained, would you still relive that day? Why or why not?
- How have you used that wisdom since that day?

Conversation SPRINGBOARD 26

Name one thing that someone in our family does for you that helps you the most.

Follow-Up Questions

- How does this help you?
- Why do you think he or she does it?
- What could he or she do to help you more?

Insight Into the Question

This question provides great insight into what teenagers perceive as being helpful, which may be different from adults' ideas.

Quick Additions

- Is there something you do that someone in our family might say helps them?
- What else could you do that would help someone in our family?
- What would you have to do to provide this help this week?
- How can I help you?

Conversation SPRINGBOARD 27

You win the lottery tomorrow—ten million dollars. What would you do with the money?

Follow-Up Questions

- How would your life change?
- Would you be happier? Explain.

Read the following passage:

Those who want to get rich fall into temptation and a trap and into many foolish and harmful desires that plunge people into ruin and destruction. For the love of money is a root of all kinds of evil. Some people, eager for money, have wandered from the faith and pierced themselves with many griefs. But you, man of God, flee from all this, and pursue righteousness, godliness, faith, love, endurance and gentleness.

1 Timothy 6:9–11

- According to this passage, what are some consequences to falling into the rich man's trap or growing eager for money?
- What advice does the final sentence (verse 11) give us?
- How could someone who is rich "flee from all this"?

Insight Into the Question

This question helps kids think about responsible spending.

Quick Additions

- If you discovered that most lottery winners went broke within five years, and some even became suicidal, would that change how you spent your money? Explain.
- What efforts would you make to be sure the money is not gone in a couple of years?
- Who might you talk to for wisdom on how to spend or invest this money?
- Would you give any away? How much, and to whom?
- What kind of impact could this make?

Conversation SPRINGBOARD 28

If someone made a movie of your life, which famous actor do you realistically think should play you?

Follow-Up Questions

- What is it about this actor that would represent you well?
- Which of your traits would you hope the actor would display? Why?
- Which of your traits would you hope the actor wouldn't reveal? Why?
- If you had a year to work on this not-so-wanted trait, could you improve it? How? (If it's something you cannot do anything about, should you be fretting over it?)

Insight Into the Question

This question helps kids self-evaluate. Hopefully yours will consider changeable attitudes and behaviors (such as anger or sarcasm) rather than characteristics she can't change, such as her cheekbones.

Quick Additions

- Which actor do you wish you were more like?
- What about him or her do you like?
- Is this a trait you think would be good for you in the long run? Why or why not?
- If so, what could you do to work toward this? Can I help?

Conversation SPRINGBOARD 29

Is there anything you'd willingly give your life for? What?

Follow-Up Questions

- Why would you sacrifice your life for this?
- How do you decide if something or someone is worth dying for?

- What does it communicate to someone if you are willing to die for him?

Insight Into the Question

This question prompts teens to dig deep into their own values. It also could open the door to conversations about Jesus and the sacrifice he made for us.

Quick Additions

- Who did Jesus die for? (John 3:16; Romans 5:8)
- What does that communicate to you?

Read the following Scripture:

God demonstrates his own love for us in this: While we were still sinners, Christ died for us.

                                                                Romans 5:8

- How does this verse describe us?
- What does this say about Jesus—that he was willing to die for a bunch of sinners?
- How does that make you feel?

Conversation SPRINGBOARD 30

Name an accomplishment you are proud of.

Follow-Up Questions

- What was the most difficult part of this accomplishment?
- Describe whether the work was worth the reward.
- Would you do it again? Why or why not?

Insight Into the Question

This question gets kids thinking about accomplishments, past and future—and what's important to them.

Quick Additions

- What is something you would like to accomplish in the future?
- What would it take to do this?
- What would you have to do this week? This month? This year?
- Can I help?

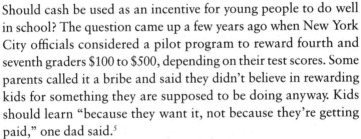

Conversation SPRINGBOARD 31

Should cash be used as an incentive for young people to do well in school? The question came up a few years ago when New York City officials considered a pilot program to reward fourth and seventh graders $100 to $500, depending on their test scores. Some parents called it a bribe and said they didn't believe in rewarding kids for something they are supposed to be doing anyway. Kids should learn "because they want it, not because they're getting paid," one dad said.[5]

What do you think?

Follow-Up Questions

- What are some good reasons for trying to do well in school?
- Would cash incentives take away from those motivations?
- For those students who don't have cash incentives, what benefits will young people get if they do well in school?
- What motivates you to do well in school?

Insight Into the Question

This controversy helps kids explore the motivations behind pursuing a good education. It may also help you as you encourage your teenager in school.

Quick Additions

- If you were in charge of education in this country, what changes would you make to your school and others, so kids would learn better?
- Why would this work better than the current system?
- Why don't they do this now?
- Could a student like you influence a change like this? How?

Conversation SPRINGBOARD 32

If you could instantly tame any animal and keep it as a pet (a lion, dolphin, bear, horse, etc.), what would you choose?

Follow-Up Questions

- What would you name it?
- What would be the most fun part of having an animal like this?
- What would be the most difficult part?
- What specific chores would this animal create for you?
- Would they be worth it? Why or why not?

Insight Into the Question

This fun question digs into your kid's imagination, providing a glimpse into his feelings about animals and an opportunity to talk about responsibilities that come with pets.

Quick Additions

- Is there a domestic (and more realistic) animal that might provide the same joy? What animal?
- What domestic pet would you like? Why?
- What would you name it?
- What chores would this create for you?
- Would it be worth it?

Conversation SPRINGBOARD 33

If you could live near the beach, or in the mountains, where would you choose? Explain.

Follow-Up Questions

- What activities would you enjoy doing at this location?
- What activities do you enjoy now that you couldn't do from this location?
- Describe where you'd want to live (in an apartment, house, camper?).

Insight Into the Question

This question not only gives you a glimpse into their personal tastes, it gets young people thinking about their futures.

Quick Additions

- What occupation would you be able to do from this location?
- What steps would you have to take to get this occupation?
- What steps are you doing right now in your life that might open the door to making this a reality?

- What actions are you taking that could hinder this from happening?

Conversation SPRINGBOARD 34

If you could freeze time and live at a certain age, what age would you stop at?

Follow-Up Questions

- What are some benefits of living life at this age?
- What would you miss out on, staying at that age?
- If you could freeze your age but no one else could—and they'd just continue growing old—would you still want to do it?

Insight Into the Question

This question prompts teens to think about what life stages they might enjoy the most.

Quick Additions

- What age would you not want to be stuck at?
- Why would this age be so bad?
- What would be some benefits of this age?

Conversation SPRINGBOARD 35

If you were stuck eating the exact same dinner for the next year, but you could choose anything you want from anywhere (you just have to eat it every night for twelve months straight), what would you choose?

Follow-Up Questions

- Why did you decide on this meal?
- How long do you think you'd last before you got sick of it?
- What is your favorite meal at home?
- What is your favorite meal when you eat out?

Insight Into the Question

This question provides a fun interaction about what foods teenagers like—always handy information when you're looking to treat your kid. ("Hey, Jake—what do you say we go to your favorite pizza place tonight?")

Quick Additions

- If you could only eat one fruit, what would it be?
- If you could only eat one vegetable, what would it be?
- If you could only have one dessert, what would you choose?
- What is one food that you'd choose to never eat again your entire life . . . and you know you'd never miss it?

Conversation SPRINGBOARD 36

What is the best birthday gift you could ever receive?

Follow-Up Questions

- Who would you want to receive it from?
- Why this item?
- How would your life change?

Insight Into the Question

This question gives you insight into what your kids want the most, and who they're close to. It can also be a door opener to talk about where true value rests.

Quick Additions

- What is the best gift you could give someone? Who would you give it to?
- Why this person?
- How do you think they would respond when they opened it?

Read the following Scripture:

My command is this: Love each other in the same way I have loved you. Greater love has no one than this: to lay down one's life for one's friends.

John 15:12–13

- What is Jesus' command?
- He tells us to love each other the way he has loved us; what ways has he shown us love?
- What does this passage say is the greatest act of love?
- Explain whether you agree or not.
- How can you show love to others this week?

Conversation SPRINGBOARD 37

What's your favorite candy sold at grocery stores or convenience stores?

Follow-Up Questions

- If you were having friends over for the evening and could buy ten snack foods, what would you choose?

- What kind of pizza would you order?
- What drinks would you serve?

Insight Into the Question

This question gives you insight into their junk food taste, which might come in handy when shopping for them on special occasions.

Quick Additions

- What is your favorite healthy snack?
- What is your favorite fruit?
- What is your favorite vegetable?

Conversation SPRINGBOARD 38

If the power went out in our city for a day (and you forgot to charge your battery-operated devices), what would you do?

Follow-Up Questions

- What would you do if there was no electricity for an entire week?
- What would you miss the most?
- How difficult would this be for you?
- Would it be good for you? Explain.

Insight Into the Question

This question gets young people thinking about their dependence on electronic gadgets and screens.

Quick Additions

- What could you gain from an experience like this?
- What would it take for you to try a gadget and media fast?
- Who in our family would have the hardest time staying away from electronic devices and media?
- Should we try it for one day? One week?

Conversation SPRINGBOARD 39

If you were going to be stranded on a desert island for a year and could only take one CD with you (a purchased CD, not one burned with personal favorites), what would you take?

Follow-Up Questions

- Why this CD?
- What is your favorite song on this CD, and why?
- How long before you'd get tired of it?

Insight Into the Question

This question gives you insight into their music taste, more than simply hearing their favorite music.

Quick Additions

- If you could make yourself just one playlist with thirty songs on it, what songs would be on that list?
- Do these songs share any common qualities?
- Would you make me that same playlist, if I was interested, or would you make some changes? Explain.
- Want to play me some of those songs now?

Conversation SPRINGBOARD 40

Why do we act on impulsive, harmful urges even when we know the result isn't good for us? We eat an extra piece of cake, knowing it's high in fat and calories. At times we are selfish or mean to people we care about, even though we know we shouldn't treat them that way. And sometimes we encounter something inappropriate on our screens, but for some reason we don't turn it off. Whatever the situation, we give in and regret it later. It's almost like we didn't see the truth . . . or didn't want to see it at the moment. It's been said, "Pleasure wins over truth." Said another way, "The temporary thrill wins over what we know is best in the long run." Why do we do this?

Follow-Up Questions

- Why don't we always focus our attention on what is best for us in the long run?
- What "temporary thrills" distract people your age?
- What distracts you from truth?

Insight Into the Question

This question gets young people thinking about the true temporary nature of many temptations they will face. It might also help them formulate a plan to avoid such distractions and steer clear of them when they surface.

Quick Additions

- We can't avoid every distraction, but sometimes we can steer clear of situations that are more tempting than others. Name some situations in which "temporary thrills" are more common.

Read the following Scripture:

Dear friends, I warn you as "temporary residents and foreigners" to keep away from worldly desires that wage war against your very souls.

1 Peter 2:11 NLT

- Why do you think Peter, the author of this verse, calls us "temporary residents" here in this world right now? (The answer you're looking for is, because our life on earth is just temporary, compared to our souls, which are eternal.)
- What does he warn us to keep away from?
- What does the verse say worldly desires do?
- Why is fulfilling our desires for a moment, not worth it in the long run?

Conversation **SPRINGBOARD 41**

What car best represents your personality?

Follow-Up Questions

- Why does this car represent you?
- Do you think other people would describe you this way?
- How would your friends describe your personality?
- What car would you like to represent your personality? Explain.

Insight Into the Question

This is a creative question to get kids thinking about how they perceive themselves and how others perceive them.

Quick Additions

- What car do you think best represents my personality?
- What about the rest of the family?

Conversation SPRINGBOARD 42

If you were the first person in the garden of Eden and had to name all the animals, pick five animals that you would rename.

Follow-Up Questions

- What would you rename these animals, and why?
- Would you want any of these animals as pets? Explain.
- If you could make a fictional animal real, which would you choose, and why?

Insight Into the Question

This question is for pure fun, and gives you insight into teens' creativity.

Quick Additions

- What is your favorite animal to watch at the zoo, and why?
- What is your best zoo memory?
- Do you want to go to the zoo again soon?

Conversation SPRINGBOARD 43

What are the top five meals your mom (dad, grandma, etc.) makes, in order?

Follow-Up Questions

- What are your top five desserts this person makes?
- Would you be interested in learning how to make any of these? Why or why not?

- When you have your own family, who is going to do the cooking in your house?

Insight Into the Question

This question provides a glimpse of your kid's taste buds—helpful information for when you want to make her something special.

Quick Additions

- What meal do you wish this person would never make again?
- What dessert do you wish this person would never make again?
- What restaurant do you never want to go to again?

Conversation **SPRINGBOARD 44**

If you could visit a fictional place for a week, where would you go?

Follow-Up Questions

- Describe what you'd want to do there.
- Is there anyone you'd hope to meet while you're there?
- Anyone you'd want to avoid?

Insight Into the Question

This question stimulates their imagination and provides you a glimpse into their favorite activities, people, and possessions.

Quick Additions

- Who would you want to take with you?

- What would you pack for this trip?
- If you could buy one item to take with you on this trip, what would you buy? Why?

Conversation **SPRINGBOARD 45**

Who do you admire the most in our immediate family?

Follow-Up Questions

- What do you admire about this person?
- Do you have this quality?
- How could you develop this quality?

Insight Into the Question

This question not only gives you a peek at who they respect, but it stimulates them to think about positive qualities they can learn and emulate.

Quick Additions

- Who is a person outside our family that you admire the most?
- What do you admire about them?
- Do you have this quality?
- How could you develop this quality?

Conversation **SPRINGBOARD 46**

A recent study showed that only 16 percent of non-Christians under age thirty say they have a "good impression" of Christianity. Think about this. That means, if you were to ask the typical young person on the street what they think of Christians, only one in six would have something good to say. One person commented: "Christianity in today's society no longer looks like Jesus."[6]

Why do you think the majority of young people have such a poor view of Christians?

Follow-Up Questions

- Do you think they are right? Explain.
- Someone said that Christians today don't look like Jesus. What do you think that person meant?
- Describe how Jesus treated others (Matthew 4:23–25, 9:35–36; Luke 23:33–43).
- How do you think crowds that encountered Jesus would have described him?
- Do most Christians today not look like Jesus? Explain.
- How would people describe you?

Insight Into the Question

This question gets young people thinking about how important it is for Christians to represent Christ.

Quick Additions

- Think about the Christians you know. Describe them.
- In what ways do they look like Jesus?
- In what ways do they not look like Jesus?
- In what ways do you look like Jesus?
- In what ways do you not look like Jesus?
- How can someone better represent Jesus (John 15:4–5)?

Conversation SPRINGBOARD 47

Half of all college students drop out before receiving a degree, according to a recent study. And one in four college freshmen don't even complete their first year.[7]
Why do you think so many college students don't finish?

Follow-Up Questions

- What are your plans for college?
- What factors might change those plans?
- What benefits are there to attending college?
- How would college help your plans for the future?

Insight Into the Question

This question gets young people thinking about their futures and the importance of college.

Quick Additions

- What do you want to major in when you are in college?
- What do you want to do after college?
- Any schooling after college? If so, what?

Conversation SPRINGBOARD 48

Every once in a while someone might sit next to you in class with a peculiar habit or irritating personality trait. What annoying mannerism bugs you the most?

Follow-Up Questions

- Why does this irritate you?

- How do you usually respond?
- Does this work?
- What do you do that might irritate others?

Insight Into the Question

This question gets kids thinking about patience and understanding.

Quick Additions

- What is the best way to deal with irritating people?
- Share about a time you didn't respond well to an irritating situation.
- Share about a time you responded really well to an irritating person.
- What advice do you think you need to hear about how to be more patient and understanding with people?

Conversation SPRINGBOARD 49

If you could go anywhere in the world for ten days, all expenses paid, where would you go?

Follow-Up Questions

- What would you want to do there?
- Who would you want to take with you, and why?
- What would you be sure to pack and take with you on this vacation?

Insight Into the Question

These questions give you insight as to not only where your kid would like to go, but who he perceives as his best friends. Do you know who your kid would choose to take on such a trip?

Quick Additions

- Is there any food you'd want to eat while on this vacation?
- Is there any food you would not want to eat while on this vacation?

Conversation SPRINGBOARD 50

If you could invent anything, what would it be, and why?

Follow-Up Questions

- How would this invention benefit society?
- How would this invention benefit you?
- Could people use this for wrong? Explain.
- Would this make you reconsider inventing it? Why or why not?

Insight Into the Question

This question prods at kids' creative sides and gives you insight into some of their interests.

Quick Additions

- What do you think was the most significant invention in history?
- How did this change the world?

- What invention would you miss the most if it were gone?
- What would you do without it?

Conversation SPRINGBOARD 51

It's Friday night, we're hanging out as a family, but we're all broke. You want to go somewhere fun, and we say, "You choose." Where could we all go and have fun for free?

Follow-Up Questions

- Would everyone like your choice? Explain.
- If you had a budget of $100, would you change your activity? What would you do?
- Which of these two nights—the free night or the $100 one—would probably be more fun? Why?

Insight Into the Question

This question sparks your teen's creativity and gives you a glimpse into her tastes in activities.

Quick Additions

- What are some fun memories you've had from "family nights"?
- What made them so fun?
- What is the next activity you would want to do as a family if you were in charge?

Conversation SPRINGBOARD 52

How much does what we see in movies affect our actions?

A large-scale study of ten- to fourteen-year-old Americans revealed that those who were exposed to many scenes of alcohol consumption in movies were more likely to experiment with alcohol or even binge-drink (which is having four or more drinks in one sitting). Young people were actually more affected by movies than by whether their parents drank or not.

Other influential factors were discovered as well, such as, if the students had friends who drank. But the influence of movies was ranked as one of the three strongest influences affecting them.[8]

Why do you think the big screen has such an effect on us?

Follow-Up Questions

• How do most movies portray drinking?
• How often do movies show consequences of heavy drinking?
• What dangers come with heavy drinking?
• Why don't movies show these dangers or consequences?

Insight Into the Question

This question gets young people thinking about the influence of the big screen, particularly in the area of drinking. Drinking is a serious issue, affecting the majority of teenagers in some way. This discussion brings Scripture into the equation, revealing God's thoughts on drunkenness.

Quick Additions

• When does drinking become wrong?
• What does the Bible say about drinking?

Read the following Scripture:

Do not get drunk on wine, which leads to debauchery. Instead, be filled with the Spirit. . . .

Ephesians 5:18

- What does this verse say about drinking?
- When does drinking become wrong?
- How do you know when you've drunk too much?

Conversation SPRINGBOARD 53

If you got lost in a foreign country for a few days, who would you want with you, and why?

Follow-Up Questions

- How would this person help you in this situation?
- What do you like most about this person?
- If you had to choose one family member to be with you during this time, who would you want with you, and why?

Insight Into the Question

This question gives you an insight into the people your teen enjoys and feels safe with in various circumstances.

Quick Additions

- Who would you want with you if you were lost for three days in the mountains, and why?
- Who would you want with you if you were lost for a day in a really tough neighborhood? Why?
- Who would you want with you if you were stranded on a desert island? Why?
- Who would you want with you if you were sad? Why?

Conversation SPRINGBOARD 54

If you had to eat at the school cafeteria, what is one item that is actually decent . . . or at least edible?

Follow-Up Questions

- What's your favorite lunch to pack?
- Which tastes better, your packed lunch, or that school cafeteria item?
- If someone stocked our refrigerator and cupboards with everything you wanted, what would you pack for a school lunch on a typical day?

Insight Into the Question

This fun question provides a peek at your teen's food preferences, especially helpful when meal choices get in a rut.

Quick Additions

- If you could throw any candy in your lunch, what would you pack?
- If you could throw any soft drink in your lunch, what would you pack?
- If you wanted a healthy lunch, what would you pack?

Conversation SPRINGBOARD 55

What is your favorite site on the Internet?

Follow-Up Questions

- What's so fun about this website?

- How much time do you think you spend on this website per day?
- Is this too much? Explain.

Insight Into the Question

This question provides insight into your teen's life on the web.

Quick Additions

- What other websites do you enjoy?
- What's a website you know I'd enjoy?
- What's a website you know I'd probably not like?
- What's a site you like, but you'd be scared to tell me you like it?

Conversation SPRINGBOARD 56

What's your favorite snack at the movie theater?

Follow-Up Questions

- If you could spend whatever you wanted at the movie theater snack bar, but you had to eat it all during the movie, what would you order?
- What do you like better, traditional theaters, drive-ins, or watching movies at home? Why?
- If you could invent a new kind of movie theater with other comforts or luxuries, what would you add?

Insight Into the Question

This is just a fun set of questions to learn about your kid's taste in movie watching.

Quick Additions

- What is one of your favorite movies?
- What is your favorite movie this year, so far?
- What movie are you looking forward to that hasn't been released yet?

Conversation SPRINGBOARD 57

What animal would describe the mood that you're in right now? Explain.

Follow-Up Questions

- Why do you think you're in this mood?
- How would you describe your typical mood?
- What is one of the biggest environmental factors that affect your mood?

Insight Into the Question

This question gives you a peek into your teen's emotions on a given day, at least how he perceives his own emotions.

Quick Additions

- Should we let external circumstances affect us? Explain.
- Who is someone you know that seems always positive regardless of the circumstances?
- What's his or her secret?
- What would it take to have this attitude?

Conversation SPRINGBOARD 58

Most people agree that schools are full of cliques or groups. Labels for these groups today include nerds, jocks, druggies . . . and even emo pandas! What are some cliques at your school?

Follow-Up Questions

- Which clique do you think people at school would place you in?
- Are they right? If not, which clique should you be in?
- What do you think of these social labels?

Insight Into the Question

This question gets young people thinking about the social circles in their school, and how they get along with them.

Quick Additions

- Which group is easiest for you to get along with?
- Which group is the most difficult for you to get along with?
- What advice would you give yourself for getting along with these difficult groups?

Conversation SPRINGBOARD 59

If you could go to any amusement park, where would you go?

Follow-Up Questions

- What would be the first thing you'd do?
- Who would you want to take with you?

- What is your favorite fun food that you could buy at this place?

Insight Into the Question

It's always fun to know places your teenager enjoys; handy information for birthdays or special occasions.

Quick Additions

- What is your favorite amusement park memory?
- What made this day so fun?

Conversation SPRINGBOARD 60

A videotape was discovered of the two Columbine killers—the two high school boys in Colorado who killed thirteen people on April 20, 1999. The two angry boys turned on the camera a month before their shooting spree and started bragging about their plans to kill everyone and how their parents didn't have a clue.

Eric and Dylan tell the story of when the Green Mountain Guns store called their home and Eric's dad answered. The clerk told him, "Your clips are in." Eric's father, who owned guns himself, told the clerk he hadn't ordered any clips. Eric tells the camera his father never asked any questions, like whether the caller even had the right phone number. Eric said that if either the clerk or his father had asked just one question, the boys would have been caught.

Eric tells another story about going to the mountains with his "terrorist bag" and how the butt of a shotgun was sticking out of it. His mother saw the gun and just assumed it was a BB gun. Eric joked how they could fool anyone, because people like his parents "didn't have a clue!"

Just over one month after making the video, the two boys killed thirteen people and wounded twenty-four, and then turned their guns on themselves in what was the most tragic school shooting of the century.

Do you think these parents should have noticed some of these clues? Explain.

Follow-Up Questions

- What could these parents have done differently?
- How much should parents be involved in the lives of their kids?
- How much is too much?

Insight Into the Question

This situation prompts young people to think about how parents might be able to help, offering guidance and even accountability.

Quick Additions

- What are some areas you wish we (your parents) would take more interest in your life?
- What are some areas you wish we would give you more space?
- How can young people earn their parents' trust?
- What are some ways you can show you are trustworthy?

Conversation SPRINGBOARD 61

If you were in a severe accident and were to lose an arm or a leg, which would you prefer? Explain.

Follow-Up Questions

- What activity would you miss the most if you lost a leg?

- If you could have a fake leg, or just no leg, which would you prefer?
- What would you miss the most if you lost your arm?
- Would you use a fake arm, or just go without?

Insight Into the Question

This question, although slightly morbid, actually helps kids appreciate some of the basic pleasures of everyday life and consider what it would be like to live with a handicap or disability.

Quick Additions

- Do you know anyone with a disability?
- What is their disability?
- How do they function with their disability?
- Do you think the disability has made them a stronger person? Why or why not?

Conversation SPRINGBOARD 62

What is your favorite item in this room, and why?

Follow-Up Questions

- If you had to get rid of this item, what would you do?
- Of all the people you know, who do you think would probably pick the same item as a favorite?
- What item do you think I would pick?

Insight Into the Question

This question gives you a peek into your kid's likes, and encourages her to think about the likes of others.

Quick Additions

- What is your favorite item in our home?
- Would you be willing to give it away if you could help a family in need?
- How would that make you feel?

Conversation SPRINGBOARD 63

It's common to have some friends who are a good influence on us and others who lead us toward trouble. Which friend or acquaintance is someone who, when you hang out with them, you actually find yourself doing good?

Follow-Up Questions

- How does this person influence you to be good?
- Why are some people drawn to hang out with trouble-makers?
- Do you think you are drawn to good influences, or trouble-makers? Explain.

The Bible talks about people who influence our morality and how Christ Jesus should be that influence.

Read the following Scripture:

Then we will no longer be immature like children. We won't be tossed and blown about by every wind of new teaching. We will not be influenced when people try to trick us with lies so clever they sound like the truth. Instead, we will speak the truth in love, growing in every way more and more like Christ, who is the head of his body, the church.

Ephesians 4:14–15 NLT

- How does the beginning of this Scripture passage describe us?
- What ways do people lie to us, or "make lies so clever they sound like the truth"?
- The passage says we can hold to the truth by becoming more like Christ. How can we become more like Christ?

Insight Into the Question

This question gets young people thinking about the friends they choose and the ramifications of the company they keep. This conversation is a good segue into discussions about the influence Jesus can have in our lives.

Quick Additions

- If your friends were asked these questions, would you be on their "good influence" list? Why or why not?
- What kind of reputation do you want?
- How can you achieve that reputation?

Conversation SPRINGBOARD 64

What's something that really irritates you?

Follow-Up Questions

- Why does this irritate you so much?
- When is the last time you experienced this?
- What did you do that particular time?

Insight Into the Question

This question provides a peek into kids' pet peeves and can help them think critically about how to respond to annoyances.

Quick Additions

- What could be done to solve this situation?
- How do people respond poorly to this kind of situation?
- How could people respond positively?
- How do you usually respond?

Conversation SPRINGBOARD 65

If you were to write a book, what would the title be?

Follow-Up Questions

- What do you have to offer about this subject?
- How would this book change our world?
- Describe the type of people who would buy this book.

Insight Into the Question

This question taps in to our kids' creativity and their God-given gifts.

Quick Additions

- Who would you choose to write the book's foreword?
- What TV talk show host should definitely interview you about this book?
- What celebrity should definitely buy your book?
- Which family member of ours could benefit the most from your book?

Conversation SPRINGBOARD 66

What chore do you despise?

Follow-Up Questions

- What do you hate about this chore?
- If you could trade for another "equal" chore, what would you choose?
- What chore do you actually enjoy (if even a little bit)?

Insight Into the Question

This question gives you insight into what chores they like and dislike, and gets them to consider the chores they deem valuable.

Quick Additions

- When you move out, will you still do these hated chores in your own home?
- What will the result be?
- Will you make your kids do the same chores you do now? What will you change?
- If money was no object but you still had to do chores, what one item could we buy to help you do a chore better?

Conversation SPRINGBOARD 67

Do wealthy kids whose parents pay for their college expenses have an advantage?

Most people would think so, but if Mommy and Daddy pay for everything, it might be a disadvantage.

A recent study revealed, "The more money parents provide for higher education, the lower the grades their children earn." The students deemed "least likely to excel" were the ones who were given essentially a blank check for college.[9]
Why do you think this is?

Follow-Up Questions

- If providing a blank check—paying for everything—is too much, how much should parents help with their kid's college expenses?
- How will this help students more than paying for everything?
- When you have children, how will you handle their college expenses?
- How will this help them?

Insight Into the Question

This question helps young people consider the ramifications of wealth.

Quick Additions

- Which would a high school student appreciate more: a car paid for with his own hard-earned money, or a brand-new car as a graduation present?
- Which would he treat better? Why?
- Which would you prefer? Why?

Conversation SPRINGBOARD 68

What song do you relate to the most?

Follow-Up Questions

- What is it about this song that you connect with?
- What kind of mood are you usually in when you choose to listen to it?
- How does the song affect your mood?
- When did you first hear this song, and how did you respond when you first heard it?

Insight Into the Question

This question uses music to talk about feelings. Music is a great discussion springboard for many young people today. They love music and often are willing to talk about it if parents are willing to approach the subject without judgment.

Quick Additions

- Is this song unique for this artist, or do you like numerous songs from this person?
- Are there other songs that connect with you in the same way? Which ones?
- If you were to put this song in a playlist, how would you title that playlist?
- What other songs would be on that list?

Conversation SPRINGBOARD 69

If you could choose a superpower (be able to fly, read minds, have superhuman strength, etc.), what would you choose?

Follow-Up Questions

- What would you do with this special gift?

- If people really had this superpower, how could they get in trouble with it?
- Do you think superpowers like this would require great responsibility from the person yielding the power?
- What are some areas in your life that you could grow to be more responsible in?

Insight Into the Question

Starting with a fun question to unleash teens' creativity, the conversation can easily shift to questions about the great responsibility that comes along with great privilege. This shouldn't turn into a lecture, but instead, be a tool to get your teen to draw her own conclusions about "responsibility."

Quick Additions

- What is a superpower no one should ever have? Why?
- What is a superpower that you think you shouldn't have? Why not?
- Would you prefer a world with superpowers, or, like our world today, no superpowers? Explain.

Conversation SPRINGBOARD 70

What Disney character is most like me?

Follow-Up Questions

- What about this character reminds you of me?
- What Disney character is most like you?
- What similarities do you have with this character?
- What about the other people in this room (in our family)— which Disney characters are they like? Explain.

Insight Into the Question

This creative question stimulates your kid to think about the character traits of family members and have a little fun with it.

Quick Additions

- Which Disney movie is your favorite?
- Which Disney character is your favorite?
- Which Disney park would you want to visit, if all expenses were paid?

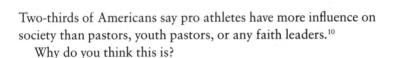

Conversation SPRINGBOARD 71

Two-thirds of Americans say pro athletes have more influence on society than pastors, youth pastors, or any faith leaders.[10]
Why do you think this is?

Follow-Up Questions

- What factors have influenced this leaning toward sports figures as role models?
- What are young people learning, or gleaning, from most sports icons?
- Why don't faith leaders have more influence?
- Who has more of an influence on you?

Insight Into the Question

This question reveals your kid's perspective on today's heroes and the influence they have.

Quick Additions

- Who are some positive sports icons?

- What are young people learning, gleaning, from this person?
- Who are some other celebrities of any kind that have a heavy influence on young people today?
- What are young people learning from these people?

Conversation SPRINGBOARD 72

If you could redecorate one room in this house, with an unlimited budget, what would you do?

Follow-Up Questions

- Why choose this particular room?
- What is the first thing you would do in the room when it was finished?
- How would life be different day to day?

Insight Into the Question

This question taps teens' creativity and gives you a peek at their personal tastes.

Quick Additions

- What would you do if you could fix up the entire house?
- How would this change life as you know it?

Conversation SPRINGBOARD 73

Who is your favorite actor or actress?

Follow-Up Questions

- What do you like about this person?
- What criteria do you use to choose a favorite actor (looks, ability, who they are when the camera is off, etc.)?
- What is your favorite movie or show with this actor?

Insight Into the Question

This question reveals their taste in celebrities and what personal characteristics they value and perhaps want to emulate.

Quick Additions

- What would you do if you happened to run into this actor or actress shopping at the grocery store?
- If this person stopped to talk with you, what would you want to ask him or her?
- What response would you hope for?

Conversation SPRINGBOARD 74

What is your favorite activity to do in the summer when school is out? Why?

Follow-Up Questions

- Who do you like to do this with, and why?
- Describe a perfect summer day, from the time you wake up to bedtime.
- What is one of your best summer memories?

Insight Into the Question

This question gives you a glimpse at what teens truly enjoy the most. It's always helpful when we know what activities and friends our kids enjoy.

Quick Additions

• Describe a perfect week in the summer.
• If you had an unlimited budget, how would this change?

Conversation SPRINGBOARD 75

Which kids are happier: those who eat whatever they want, drink alcohol, and smoke, or those who eat healthy foods and live a healthier lifestyle?

A recent study suggests an unhealthy lifestyle is linked to unhappiness. In fact, in their analysis of five thousand young people between the ages of ten and fifteen, researchers discovered:

• Young people who never drank alcohol were four to six times more likely to have higher levels of happiness than those who consumed alcohol.
• Youth who smoked were about five times less likely to have high happiness scores compared to those who never smoked.
• Higher consumption of fruit and vegetables and lower consumption of chips, sweets, and soft drinks were both associated with high happiness.
• The more hours of sports that young people participated in per week, the happier they were.[11]

Why do you think this is the case?

Follow-Up Questions

- Do you think young people today are attracted to the idea of being able to do whatever they like?
- What are some consequences of unhealthy eating, drinking, or smoking?
- Explain why "doing whatever you like" actually isn't as rewarding as expected?

Insight Into the Question

This question helps young people consider the sources of happiness.

Quick Additions

- What makes young people truly happy? Why?
- What makes you happy? Why?
- How can you avoid falling into the "do whatever I like" trap?

Conversation SPRINGBOARD 76

If an editor from the local newspaper called and said they would publish an article from you on the front page tomorrow, no matter the topic, what would you write about?

Follow-Up Questions

- Why would you write about that?
- Who would you hope would read it?
- How would you hope people would respond?

Insight Into the Question

This question might give you a peek at your child's interests, and even reveal his passions and motivations.

Quick Additions

- What is the best thing you've ever written?
- If you had the choice of writing an article for the newspaper, drawing a comic strip, or delivering the papers, which would you choose, and why?
- Which do you prefer: blogging, tweeting, or posting a pic?

Conversation SPRINGBOARD 77

What's the most encouraging thing someone ever said to you?

Follow-Up Questions

- Why did this make you feel so good?
- How did you respond?
- Why do you think they told you this?

Insight Into the Question

This question helps kids recall a time when they were encouraged and built up.

Quick Additions

- What is the most encouraging thing you have ever told someone?
- How did they respond?
- Why did you tell them this?
- How did it make you feel?

- What is something encouraging you could tell someone this week?

Conversation **SPRINGBOARD 78**

If you were the final deciding vote on whose face was to go on a new coin, who would you choose?

Follow-Up Questions

- Why does this person deserve to be on a coin?
- How much should this coin be worth?
- What criteria should our country use to decide who is on our coins?

Insight Into the Question

This silly question gives kids a chance to consider who is worthy of honor.

Quick Additions

- If you could put family members on coins, who would go on which coins?
- If you could put your face on a bill of any denomination, what denomination would you want to be on, and why?

Conversation **SPRINGBOARD 79**

What is one thing God has been teaching you lately?

Follow-Up Questions

- How is this changing you?

- Describe a situation where you've been learning this.
- How will you approach this situation next time?

Insight Into the Question

This question helps kids reflect on God and his work in their lives.

Quick Additions

- What are some ways we can receive God's instruction?
- Which of these sources do you like the best?

Conversation **SPRINGBOARD 80**

If a natural disaster hit our house and you only had time to grab one item before fleeing, what would you choose?

Follow-Up Questions

- Why is this item so special to you?
- Five years ago, what would you have grabbed?
- What do you think you'll grab in five years from now?

Insight Into the Question

This question gives you insight into the possessions she cherishes, and may reveal how our values can change.

Quick Additions

- If you had time to grab three items, what would they be?
- Why are these items so special?
- What items do you think the rest of the family would grab, and why?

Conversation SPRINGBOARD 81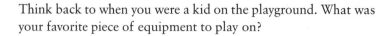

Think back to when you were a kid on the playground. What was your favorite piece of equipment to play on?

Follow-Up Questions

• Share a memory you have of playing on this.
• Why do you think you liked it so much?
• When did you finally get tired of it? Why?

Insight Into the Question

This nostalgic question prompts teens to reflect on fond childhood memories.

Quick Additions

• What games did you like to play during recess at school?
• Who were some of the friends you used to play with?

Conversation SPRINGBOARD 82

Where do you realistically see yourself in ten years?

Follow-Up Questions

• Describe a typical day in your life ten years from now.
• What will you have to accomplish in the next ten years for this to happen?
• What could interfere with these plans?

Insight Into the Question

This question helps kids think about their futures and the effects of today's decisions.

Quick Additions

- It doesn't have to be realistic, but dream where it would be fun to be in ten years, if nothing would get in your way!
- Is there any way this would actually be possible? What would it take?
- What would you have to do tomorrow, next week, and next month to make this happen?

Conversation **SPRINGBOARD 83**

Who's worse about texting while driving, teenagers or adults?

The answer might surprise you.

We've all heard the news that teenagers keep texting while driving. But according to a recent survey by AT&T, more adults admit to texting and driving than do teenagers. Of teenagers, 43 percent admit to texting and driving, while 49 percent of adults do. And 98 percent of adults say they know it's wrong but do it anyway. Six in ten say they weren't texting while driving three years ago.[12]

What is the biggest problem here?

Follow-Up Questions

- Do you think more adults text while driving, or do just think more adults admit it? Explain.
- If 98 percent of adults think it's wrong to do it, why do you think exactly half of them do it anyway?
- Why do we sometimes do things we don't want to do?

Insight Into the Question

This question provokes kids to think about human nature and the tendency to rebel against what we know is best for ourselves in the long run.

Quick Additions

Read the following passage:

For I have the desire to do what is good, but I cannot carry it out. For I do not do the good I want to do, but the evil I do not want to do—this I keep on doing.

Romans 7:18–19

- In these verses, the apostle Paul sounds frustrated. What does he have the desire to do?
- But what does he keep doing instead?
- Share a time when you felt like this. What did you do?

In the next chapter of Romans, Paul explains how we need to stop living with our minds set on these earthly desires, but instead focus our minds on what God's spirit desires (verse 5).

- What is the best way to focus our mind on what God desires?

Conversation SPRINGBOARD 84

If you could take one person on a cross-country road trip, who would it be?

Follow-Up Questions

- Why this person?

- What states would you want to make sure to drive through, and what sights would you want to visit?
- Where would you stay each night? How much would this cost?

Insight Into the Question

This question reveals who our kids like to spend time with and a bit about their travel tastes.

Quick Additions

- What would be the best part of this trip?
- What would be the worst part of this trip?
- Would you like to do a trip like this someday? When? Explain.

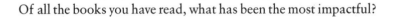

Conversation **SPRINGBOARD 85**

Of all the books you have read, what has been the most impactful?

Follow-Up Questions

- How did it impact you?
- What specifically did you like about this book?
- Has this book changed the way you think or act? In what ways?

Insight Into the Question

This question gives you a glimpse into teens' tastes in literature.

Quick Additions

- Name three other books you really enjoy.

- If you could either read a book this good, or watch a good movie, which would you choose? Why?
- Name a book that you enjoyed but didn't like the movie.
- Name a book for which both the book and movie were good.

Conversation SPRINGBOARD 86

If you could have a $100 gift certificate to any store, what store would you choose?

Follow-Up Questions

- Why this store?
- What would you probably buy?
- How would your life change when you had this item?
- Do you think you'd still be using this item in a year? In five years?

Insight Into the Question

This is a creative way to learn where teens would like to shop and the items they are drawn to.

Quick Additions

- What would you buy if you had a $500 gift certificate for this store?
- What would you buy if you had $1,000 to spend at this store?
- What store would be second on your list to shop at?

Conversation **SPRINGBOARD 87**

If you could collect $10,000 now, or wait two years for $20,000, which would you choose? Explain.

Follow-Up Questions

- If you took the $10,000 now, how would you spend it?
- If you waited two years for $20,000, how would you spend it then?
- Why would it be smart to wait the two years?
- Why would many people take the $10,000 now?

Insight Into the Question

This question reveals whether your kid believes in delayed gratification.

Quick Additions

- Would you say you are a spender or a saver?
- What is the most money you've ever saved? Did you eventually purchase something with this? What?
- What is something you'd like to save for now?
- What sacrifices would you have to make now to save for this?

Conversation **SPRINGBOARD 88**

You achieve something for which our whole family wants to take you somewhere fun to eat and celebrate with you. Perhaps you got straight As, hit a home run, or sang well during a performance. Where would you want to celebrate?

Follow-Up Questions

- Why this place?
- What would you order?
- If you've been to this place before, what is a good memory you have here?

Insight Into the Question

This question not only gives you an idea of fun places your kid likes to eat, but also provides a glimpse at fun memories.

Quick Additions

- What are two other places to eat that are fun like this?
- What is fun about these places?
- What would you order at these places?

Conversation SPRINGBOARD 89

What is the best dream you can remember?

Follow-Up Questions

- What made this dream so good?
- What was your worst nightmare?
- What is the most recent dream you can remember?

Insight Into the Question

If you think about it, we spend more time in bed than most other activities. These questions dive into dreams, as well as sleep habits and preferences.

Quick Additions

- Describe how you are most comfortable sleeping (example: "on my stomach while hugging my pillow . . .").
- How many times do you usually wake up at night? Do you go right back to sleep?
- Is there anything that helps you go to sleep (soft music, a fan, counting sheep . . .)?

Conversation SPRINGBOARD 90

Why do you think young people go to tanning salons?

There's no question tanning is popular. In one study, almost half of young women and a little more than a quarter of guys said they actively try to get a tan from the sun, regardless of warnings they hear about skin cancer or UV exposure. When the tanning habits of four hundred college students aged eighteen to twenty-four were examined, 27 percent showed signs of "tanorexia"—with students craving the sun or a tanning bed "in much the same way addicts yearn for alcohol or drugs."

Researchers concluded, "People value attractiveness and they're willing to take health risks to be attractive."[13]

Do you think this is true with the people you know?

Follow-Up Questions

- Why do people desire tans?
- How much do you value a tan?
- When does the desire for a tan become excessive?
- When does "fear of sunburn" become too excessive?

Insight Into the Question

This question gets teens to think about the lengths people will go to feel good about themselves.

Quick Additions

- What other ways do people try to improve their looks?
- When does this become unhealthy?
- What ways do you try to improve your looks?
- Does this ever become unhealthy?

Conversation SPRINGBOARD 91

Favorite milk shake. What flavor, and from where?

Follow-Up Questions

- How do you drink milk shakes (spoon, straw, etc.)?
- Which way do you prefer your ice cream the most (shake, cone, sundae, etc.)?
- Share a fun ice-cream-eating memory.

Insight Into the Question

A fun question that provides handy information for when you want to treat your teen. It may also lead to a good story or two.

Quick Additions

- If an ice-cream truck pulled up in front, what would you get?
- Baskin-Robbins—what flavor?
- At a yogurt shop, what's your favorite flavor and toppings?
- At an ice-cream mix-it shop (such as Cold Stone Creamery), what's your go-to mixture?

Conversation SPRINGBOARD 92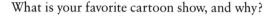

What is your favorite cartoon show, and why?

Follow-Up Questions

- Who is your favorite character on the show, and why?
- Who is your least favorite character on the show, and why?

Insight Into the Question

This question gives you a peek into their taste of entertainment and what personal traits they are drawn to.

Quick Additions

- If you could hang out with a cartoon character, who would you choose?
- Why him or her?
- Which cartoon character are you most like? How are you similar?

Conversation SPRINGBOARD 93

If you could watch a video showing the actual footage of *any* event in history (signing of the Declaration of Independence, your birth, the building of Noah's ark, etc.), which event would you pick?

Follow-Up Questions

- Why this event?
- What would you hope to see?
- How does this event impact your world today?

Insight Into the Question

This question gives you insight into your kid's history knowledge and interests.

Quick Additions

- If you could step in and influence this event in history, what would you want to do?
- How would that change history?
- Could changing this event have bad repercussions? Explain.

Conversation SPRINGBOARD 94

Where would you want to go for a family vacation?

Follow-Up Questions

- What would you want to do at this place?
- How long would you like to stay?
- If you could take one friend with you, who would it be?

Insight Into the Question

This question reveals what kids value about vacations.

Quick Additions

- Describe a fun family vacation memory.
- What made this so special?
- What kind of vacations do you hope to take your own family on when you are out on your own?

Conversation **SPRINGBOARD 95**

What is something funny a close friend or family member does that always makes you laugh?

Follow-Up Questions

- What movie made you laugh?
- What TV show always makes you laugh?
- What book made you laugh?

Insight Into the Question

This question reveals what teens find funny, which can be different from what adults think is funny.

Quick Additions

- What is a fun memory you have of laughing?
- Describe a time when you laughed so hard your sides hurt.
- Where are you ticklish?

Conversation **SPRINGBOARD 96**

If the president of our country came to our house for dinner and asked you what one change you'd like to see, what would you tell him?

Follow-Up Questions

- Why would you choose this?
- How do you hope he'd respond?
- How would the world change if he put policies in place to make that change?

Insight Into the Question

This question gets young people thinking about causes they support.

Quick Additions

- If you were president, what would you do differently?
- How would this change our country?
- Do you think people would vote for you again? Why?
- Is there any way you can help make this positive change, even in small ways? How?

Conversation SPRINGBOARD 97

No one likes to be lied to. We value people who are real and authentic. Sadly, sometimes we aren't even real to ourselves. This isn't anything new. Famous nineteenth-century novelist Fyodor Dostoyevsky (1821–1881) wrote, "Lying to ourselves is more deeply ingrained than lying to others." Do you think he is right? Explain.

Follow-Up Questions

- What is an example of someone lying to himself?
- Why would people lie to themselves?
- Describe a situation where someone you know, or know about, didn't want to see the truth.

Insight Into the Question

This question gets young people thinking about being honest with themselves.

Quick Additions

- What is a common problem people tend to ignore about themselves?
- What is a problem that you sometimes find yourself ignoring about yourself?
- When does ignoring a problem grow into full-blown denial?
- What are some common consequences of denial?
- What is a good way we can address problems outright instead of allowing them to grow into denial?

Conversation SPRINGBOARD 98

What did you get into trouble for most often when you were younger?

Follow-Up Questions

- How do remember us (your parents) responding?
- Was our response or punishment fair?
- How would you respond if your kid did that?

Insight Into the Question

This question gives teens the opportunity to reflect on their childhood and then give parenting advice. Their perspectives on situations can be much different from ours.

Quick Additions

- What's the worst thing you remember getting in trouble for?
- What was your punishment?
- Was it fair?
- Did you learn your lesson? Explain.

Conversation **SPRINGBOARD 99**

Who has been your favorite teacher, and why?

Follow-Up Questions

- What is one thing you learned from this teacher?
- Describe a typical day in class with this teacher.
- What's more important in a teacher: the ability to teach well, or the way he or she interacts with students? Explain.

Insight Into the Question

This question gives you a little insight into teens' opinions of their teachers and the qualities they like in good teachers.

Quick Additions

- Who is one of the worst teachers you've had?
- If you were a teacher, how would you teach differently?
- What is the most important skill or character trait you'd look for if you were hiring a teacher?

Conversation **SPRINGBOARD 100**

How do you think we (your family) would describe you first thing in the morning?

Follow-Up Questions

- Are we right? What is the truth?
- What time of day are you the happiest, and why?
- What time of day are you the grumpiest, and why?

- Is there something that could be done to improve this lousy time of the day?

Insight Into the Question

This question helps kids think about their attitudes and behaviors throughout the day.

Quick Additions

- Who in this family has an attitude most like yours?
- How would you describe that person first thing in the morning?
- What could you do to improve that lousy time of the day for him?

Conversation SPRINGBOARD 101

Describe one of the most embarrassing moments in your life.

Follow-Up Questions

- How did people respond?
- How did you walk away from the situation?
- Now that's it's over, is it funny, painful, or just still embarrassing? Explain.
- Did this moment change how you approach similar situations?

Insight Into the Question

This question invites teens to be a bit vulnerable by reflecting on embarrassing moments, and can lead to good talks about different responses when things don't go our way.

Quick Additions

- Describe a time when you were embarrassed for someone else.
- How did you respond?

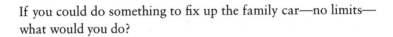

Conversation SPRINGBOARD 102

If you could do something to fix up the family car—no limits— what would you do?

Follow-Up Questions

- How would this change family trips?
- Who else in our family might like these changes the most?
- Who would like these changes the least?
- How would you fix up the family car differently if you were trying to please everyone?

Insight Into the Question

This question taps in to kids' creativity and gives you a peek at their taste in automobiles.

Quick Additions

- If you had $40,000 and could buy a new family car, what would you buy?
- What color?
- Where is the first place you'd want to go in the car?

Conversation SPRINGBOARD 103

What do you like to do to relax?

Follow-Up Questions

- What is one of your best memories related to this activity?
- Do you get enough of this form of relaxation? Too much? Explain.
- How do you feel after relaxing this way?

Insight Into the Question

This question explores the topic of "rest" and, when your teen is feeling stressed or overwhelmed, can provide you insights to help her relax.

Quick Additions

- What do you think God's opinion is about relaxation and rest?

Read the following passage:

"Six days you shall labor, but on the seventh day you shall rest; even during the plowing season and harvest you must rest."

Exodus 34:21

- What does God tell us to do on the seventh day?
- Why do you think God tells us this?
- Why do you think God specifically mentioned "even during the plowing season and harvest you must rest"?
- How does living this way look for you?

Conversation SPRINGBOARD 104

A few years ago the Tennessee state legislature started requiring DUI offenders to pick up trash on roadsides wearing neon-colored vests with huge letters, reading, "I AM A DRUNK DRIVER."[14] Many people were skeptical of the effectiveness of this shaming technique. Do you think it would work on most people?

Follow-Up Questions

- Is it ever okay to shame someone for their actions? Explain.
- What do you think is an adequate punishment for drunk drivers?
- Is a drunk driver who accidentally kills someone worse than a drunk driver who gets home with no accident and not being arrested? Explain.

Insight Into the Question

This question gets young people thinking about choices and consequences.

Quick Additions

- Why do you think people get behind the wheel of a car when they're drunk?
- What are some consequences to driving under the influence?
- How important is it to give people consequences for their actions? Why?

Conversation SPRINGBOARD 105

What is one thing you can do that no other family member can do?

Follow-Up Questions

- When did you learn, or first notice, this ability or skill?
- What benefit is this ability or skill?
- What can a family member do that you wish you could do? Why?

Insight Into the Question

This question helps teens think about their own abilities and skills, as well as skills they'd like to acquire.

Quick Additions

- What talent or skill does one of your friends have that you'd like to have? Why?
- What would it take to be able to do this?
- Are you willing to work at it?
- What would you have to do this week or this month to begin?

Conversation SPRINGBOARD 106

What is an impactful lesson you learned from the natural consequences of an action?

Follow-Up Questions

- How did your behavior change the next time?
- Why are natural consequences such an effective teaching tool?
- How can parents use natural consequences to teach their kids?

Insight Into the Question

This question gets kids thinking about the consequences of their actions and the lessons learned.

Quick Additions

- What are some consequences we (your parents) imposed that you really deserved?
- What consequence did we impose that you think was unfair?
- How would you have handled the situation differently if you were the parent?

Conversation SPRINGBOARD 107

What is a movie everybody hated, but you liked?

Follow-Up Questions

- What did you like about the movie?
- Is there any truth to people's dislike of the movie? Explain.
- How could the film makers have made it better?

Insight Into the Question

This fun question not only gives you a glimpse into your teen's taste in entertainment, it encourages critical thinking.

Quick Additions

- What is a movie everyone liked, but you hated?
- What did you dislike about this film?
- How could the film makers have made it better?
- What is a good film, with a similar storyline or in the same genre, that people should see instead of the one you hated?

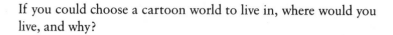

Conversation SPRINGBOARD 108

If you could choose a cartoon world to live in, where would you live, and why?

Follow-Up Questions

- What is the first thing you would do in this cartoon world?
- Who would you hope to encounter in this cartoon world?
- What would be the scariest part of this cartoon world?

Insight Into the Question

This question taps in to your teen's creativity.

Quick Additions

- If an artist drew you as a cartoon character, describe how she would draw you.
- What clothes would you be wearing as a 'toon?
- What cartoon companion would be with you in this cartoon?

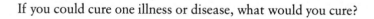

Conversation SPRINGBOARD 109

If you could cure one illness or disease, what would you cure?

Follow-Up Questions

- Why this one?
- Describe what the world would be like without this.
- In reality, is there any way people can steer clear of this illness or disease? Explain.

Insight Into the Question

This question prompts kids to think compassionately about people dealing with illnesses and diseases around the world.

Quick Additions

- What is the most sick you've ever been?
- Who took care of you?
- How do you like to be pampered when you're sick?
- What is something you could do for others when they are sick?

Conversation SPRINGBOARD 110

If people are hateful toward you, is there anything you can do to change them?

Dr. Martin Luther King Jr. wrote, "Darkness cannot drive out darkness; only light can do that. Hate cannot drive out hate; only love can do that."[15]

Is he right?

Follow-Up Questions

- Why do you think he parallels darkness to hate?
- Explain how love drives out hate.
- Give an example.

Insight Into the Question

This question helps kids think about the power of love. If you want, you can also use this to springboard a discussion about Jesus.

Quick Additions

Read the following passage:

But when the Pharisees heard about the miracle, they said, "No wonder he can cast out demons. He gets his power from Satan, the prince of demons."

Jesus knew their thoughts and replied, "Any kingdom divided by civil war is doomed. A town or family splintered by feuding will fall apart. And if Satan is casting out Satan, he is divided and fighting against himself. His own kingdom will not survive. And if I am empowered by Satan, what about your own exorcists? They cast out demons, too, so they will condemn you for what you have said. But if I am casting out demons by the Spirit of God, then the Kingdom of God has arrived among you. For who is powerful enough to enter the house of a strong man like Satan and plunder his goods? Only someone even stronger—someone who could tie him up and then plunder his house.

Matthew 12:24–29 NLT

- What did the Pharisees accuse Jesus of?
- What argument does Jesus use in the last two sentences (verse 29) to retort?
- What does that mean?
- How does Dr. Martin Luther King Jr.'s speech parallel this?
- How can you drive away hate with love this week?

Conversation **SPRINGBOARD 111**

What is one irrational fear you have?

Follow-Up Questions

- Why is this fear irrational?
- Is there any truth behind the fear at all? Explain.
- What is a way you can overcome this fear?

- When is fear a good thing?
- When is fear a bad thing?

Insight Into the Question

This question encourages young people to examine their fears. Fear can be a good thing—like the fear of putting oneself into a dangerous situation. But some of our fears are irrational, like being afraid of monsters under our beds.

Quick Additions

- What is a rational fear you have?
- How do you usually respond when you're in this situation?
- Why do you think God created us to be afraid in dangerous situations?

Conversation SPRINGBOARD 112

Describe one of your favorite memories.

Follow-Up Questions

- What is so special about this?
- What elements of this situation could happen again?
- Could something like this happen again?
- Do you have the power to create situations that will become favorite memories? Explain.

Insight Into the Question

This nostalgic question gets kids thinking about fun memories and examining how to pursue positive activities.

Quick Additions

- What is something you plan on doing in the near future that might become one of your favorite memories?
- What will be so special about this?
- Which people in your life help make good memories?

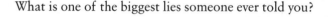

Conversation SPRINGBOARD 113

What is one of the biggest lies someone ever told you?

Follow-Up Questions

- Did you believe that person at first? What happened?
- How did you finally figure out you had been lied to?
- What was your first impulse when you discovered the truth?
- How did you respond?
- Looking back at the situation, do you wish you would have responded differently? How?

Insight Into the Question

This question helps kids look introspectively at a situation in which someone lied to them. Hopefully this will stimulate ideas on how they can respond to this common experience next time.

Quick Additions

- What is one of the biggest lies you ever told?
- How long did it take, if ever, before the truth was discovered?
- How did you feel when you first lied?
- How did you feel later?
- If you had to do the situation over again, what would you do?

Conversation SPRINGBOARD 114

What was your favorite toy when you were young?

Follow-Up Questions

- What was your favorite thing to do with this toy?
- How old were you when you got it, and how long did you use it or keep it?
- Why do you think you finally lost interest in it?
- What toy or gadget or device do you have right now that you'll probably tire of soon? Why?

Insight Into the Question

This fun question is a drive down memory lane, with a few stops to think about materialism.

Quick Additions

- What toy did you always want but never got?
- Why didn't you ever get it?
- How would your life have been different if you had it?

Conversation SPRINGBOARD 115

If you could go back and change one decision you made this past week, what would you change, and why?

Follow-Up Questions

- How would your week have changed?
- How did the situation turn out in reality?

- How could you realistically be careful to make your preferred choice in the future?

Insight Into the Question

This question gets teens thinking about choices, consequences, and more importantly, good decision-making in the future.

Quick Additions

- What is a decision you made this week that you are proud of and you would not change?
- How did this situation turn out?
- How could it have turned badly if you chose differently?

Conversation SPRINGBOARD 116

A recent study examined the relation between frequency of family dinners and mental health. In other words, is it good for families to eat meals together?
What do you think?

Follow-Up Questions

- What are some benefits of eating together as a family?
- What do you guess that researchers discovered in this study?

Researchers discovered, "More frequent family dinners related to fewer emotional and behavioral problems, greater emotional well-being, more trusting and helpful behaviors towards others, and higher life satisfaction." Furthermore, these family meal times with "social exchanges" benefitted the adolescents' well-being "regardless of whether or not they feel they can easily talk to their parents."[16]

- Why do you think more frequent family dinners were related to all these positive outcomes?
- Why are social exchanges with parents important?

Insight Into the Question

This question helps young people examine the benefits of eating together as a family.

Quick Additions

- Describe the perfect family mealtime.
- What would make family mealtimes better?
- What would make social exchanges with us (your parents) better?
- Why do you think this study discovered that social exchanges were good for kids even if the kids didn't think it was easy to talk with their parents?

Conversation SPRINGBOARD 117

What is something you do differently than most people?

Follow-Up Questions

- Why do you do it differently?
- How does it usually turn out?
- Would you like to keep doing it your way, or do you think you should change it? Why?

Insight Into the Question

This question helps kids examine some of their own behaviors.

Quick Additions

- What is something a family member does differently than you?
- How does it usually turn out, compared to the way you do it?
- Which way is better? Explain.
- Is it a matter of fact, or an opinion, or "style"? Explain.

Conversation SPRINGBOARD 118

Do you ever wish you had a twin? Why or why not?

Follow-Up Questions

- How would your life be different?
- Would you want an identical twin, or a fraternal twin?
- If fraternal, guy or girl?
- What would his or her name be?

Insight Into the Question

This question is pure fun, but also gives you an insight into your teen's imagination and how she views sibling relationships.

Quick Additions

- What is the perfect number of brothers and sisters? Why?
- How would life be different for you if you had three more siblings than you currently have?
- How would life be different if you were an only child?
- What are some positive aspects of your current situation?

Conversation **SPRINGBOARD 119**

What is the last thing you cried about?

Follow-Up Questions

- How often do you cry?
- What does it take to bring you to tears?
- Which is better, crying or holding in your emotions? Why?

Insight Into the Question

This question examines kids' reactions to tough times. Try to help your teen understand that crying is okay and bottling up feelings isn't healthy.

Quick Additions

- How do you respond when you see a friend crying?
- How does this help?
- How would you like someone to respond when you're crying?

Conversation **SPRINGBOARD 120**

What is the best gift you've ever given someone?

Follow-Up Questions

- How did he or she respond?
- How did it make you feel to give this gift?
- Why is it fun to give?
- What is more fun, giving or receiving? Explain.

Insight Into the Question

This question stimulates young people to think about the gifts they've given and received.

Quick Additions

- What is the best gift you've ever received?
- Why was this so amazing?
- Could you ever give a similar gift? Explain.

Conversation SPRINGBOARD 121

If you were to plug in your phone or music player to our stereo, pull up your entire music library and hit shuffle, which song would you be most nervous about and hope would not play during a family dinner?

Follow-Up Questions

- Why would you be nervous about this song?
- Why do you have this song?
- What is the message of this song?
- Do you think you should even have this song? Why or why not?

Insight Into the Question

This question gives kids a chance to be honest about their music and think through song lyrics. If you want your teen to open up and answer this question honestly, you'll have to create an environment where he trusts your reaction. Here's a good chance for you to turn what could be an overreaction into an interaction. It's okay to have rules and say, "This doesn't belong in our house," but try to teach him the process of discernment, rather than just being the "no" parent.

Quick Additions

- Which of your songs do you think I'd like if I just gave it a chance?
- Which song do you wish I'd like, but you know I won't like?
- How much do you think music content affects you?

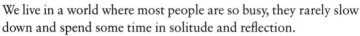

Conversation SPRINGBOARD 122

We live in a world where most people are so busy, they rarely slow down and spend some time in solitude and reflection.

Philosopher Albert Camus said, "In order to understand the world, one has to turn away from it on occasion."[17]

What did he mean by this?

Follow-Up Questions

- Do you agree with the philosopher's quote? Explain.
- Why would a time of rest and solitude possibly help?
- What is the result if we never slow down and rest?

Insight Into the Question

This question gets teens thinking about the need for rest. Be careful, though, this is an area where we'd better be able to practice what we preach.

Quick Additions

- What are some great ways to "unplug" and truly relax from the busyness of the world?
- Do you think unplugging electrical devices and turning off your phone for a couple of hours could be a good thing? Explain.

- What are ways you think we (your parents) could better relax?

Conversation SPRINGBOARD 123

If you could go back in time and give yourself one piece of advice before high school (or middle school), what advice would you offer?

Follow-Up Questions

- Why this advice?
- Would you have listened?
- How would your life have changed if you had?
- Is it too late now? Could you still use this advice? Explain.

Insight Into the Question

This question helps teens think through past decisions and give themselves advice.

Quick Additions

- What piece of advice do you need "future you" to come back and give to you right now?
- Why do you need this advice?
- Will you listen? Why or why not?
- How will this help you?

Conversation SPRINGBOARD 124

What is the biggest misconception people have about teenagers?

Follow-Up Questions

- What is the truth of the matter?
- Why do people think this way?
- How could teenagers change this stigma?

Insight Into the Question

This question helps kids consider their reputations and think strategically about how to change them for the better.

Quick Additions

- What is the biggest misconception teens have about adults?
- Do you think there's any truth to this misconception? Explain.
- What could adults do to change this impression?

Conversation **SPRINGBOARD 125**

Finish this sentence: "My life would be better if . . ."

Follow-Up Questions

- Describe what would change if this became true.
- Why would this be better for you?
- Is this an achievable wish? If so, what would it take to achieve it?

Insight Into the Question

Young people either answer this with attainable desires, such as "to get better grades" or "treat people better," or they respond with wishful thinking, such as "I wish I were six inches taller." Obviously the conversation will go a different route depending on their answers. If you get a realistic response, gain even more insights by rephrasing the questions to hear wishful responses (and vice versa).

Quick Additions

- Who is someone you know who is this (or has this)?
- Do you look up to this person?
- What kind of influence does this person have on you?

Conversation SPRINGBOARD 126

What is your favorite smell?

Follow-Up Questions

- Why is this smell so good?
- What was the worst odor you have smelled recently?
- When do you use your nose—your sense of smell—most often?

Insight Into the Question

This question stimulates kids to tap in to their senses and examine something they use every day.

Quick Additions

- What is your favorite sound? Why?
- What sound do you hate? Why?

Conversation SPRINGBOARD 127

Would you rather have a great job and live in a big house but be totally alone, or have a meager job, struggling to make a living, but surrounded by friends and family? Why?

Follow-Up Questions

- How important is it for you to be connected with family?
- How important is it for you to be connected with your friends?
- What part do riches and possessions have in all of this?

Insight Into the Question

This question gives you a peek at what your kid values more: money and stability, or relationships.

Quick Additions

- If you did own a meager little house, what are three features or amenities you'd want?
- If you had to cut one of these, what would go?

Conversation SPRINGBOARD 128

If you had to live either in Arizona, where it's scorching hot most of the year, or in Alaska, where it's below freezing for many months, which would you choose? Why?

Follow-Up Questions

- What do you enjoy doing in a hot climate?
- What do you enjoy doing in a cold climate?

- If you could live in both climates during the year, what percentage of the year would you want to live in each? Explain.

Insight Into the Question

This fun question reveals a little about teens' weather preferences, and also brings out their ideas about personal comfort.

Quick Additions

- What is the perfect outdoors warm temperature? Why?
- What is the perfect outdoors cold temperature? Why?
- If you had to pick one climate to live in year around—living in a place that stays the exact same temperature—what temperature would you choose?

Conversation SPRINGBOARD 129

What would be your choice breakfast to start the day?

Follow-Up Questions

- If someone were to fix you breakfast every morning, would you prefer a big breakfast or just a small snack?
- What did you have for breakfast the last five mornings?
- Which is your favorite meal of the day?

Insight Into the Question

This question is a fun way to learn a bit more about your kid's food preferences, which often change during the teen years, and also which meals are important to her.

Quick Additions

- What is your favorite restaurant for breakfast?
- What do you order there?
- What is your favorite lunch place?
- What do you order there?
- What is your favorite dinner restaurant?
- What do you eat there?

Conversation SPRINGBOARD 130

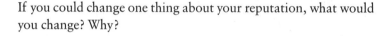

If you could change one thing about your reputation, what would you change? Why?

Follow-Up Questions

- What would you have to do to change?
- How did you get this reputation?
- Is this true to who you really are inside?

Insight Into the Question

This question helps kids think about how they are perceived by others. It's healthy to think about how our actions affect others, but it's unhealthy to obsess about what others think of us. Hopefully these conversations can help your teen find a balance.

Quick Additions

- What's the difference between having a good reputation and being worried about what people think?
- When does concern about your reputation become obsessing over what people think?

- Who is someone you know who balances this well? Explain how they demonstrate this.

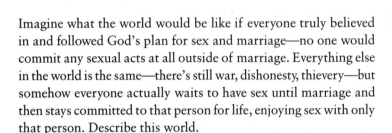

Conversation **SPRINGBOARD 131**

Imagine what the world would be like if everyone truly believed in and followed God's plan for sex and marriage—no one would commit any sexual acts at all outside of marriage. Everything else in the world is the same—there's still war, dishonesty, thievery—but somehow everyone actually waits to have sex until marriage and then stays committed to that person for life, enjoying sex with only that person. Describe this world.

Follow-Up Questions

- Would there be any sexually transmitted diseases? Why?
- Would there be any rape, incest, or molestation? Why?
- Would there be any divorce? Why?
- Would there be any pornography, or prostitution? Why?

Insight Into the Question

This question gets young people thinking about how amazing God's plan for sex really is, as opposed to the world's "anything goes" attitude toward sex. It's mindboggling how many natural consequences can be avoided when we put our trust in God's way in this one simple area.

Quick Additions

- Why do you think people aren't willing to trust God's plan for sex and marriage?
- What would people "miss out on" if they trusted God in this area of their lives?
- What would people gain?

Conversation **SPRINGBOARD 132**

Almost all of us have laughed so hard at times that we cried. When is the last time you experienced this?

Follow-Up Questions

• Why do you think this triggered this reaction out of you?
• What usually makes you laugh?
• Who usually makes you laugh?

Insight Into the Question

This question examines what makes your kids laugh.

Quick Additions

• What is one of the funniest movies you've seen?
• What is one of the funniest jokes you've heard?
• Who is the funniest comedian you've heard?

Conversation **SPRINGBOARD 133**

If you could bring one person back to life and hang with them for just a day, who would you choose? Why?

Follow-Up Questions

• What would you want to do with this person?
• What would you hope to talk about?
• What would be nice to hear from this person?

Insight Into the Question

This question gives you a glimpse into your child's knowledge of history and the issues he cares about.

Quick Additions

- Which ancestor do you wish you could meet? Why?
- Which person in history do you wish you could meet? Why?
- Which biblical character do you wish you could meet? Why?

Conversation SPRINGBOARD 134

What is your favorite season, and why?

Follow-Up Questions

- What are some of your favorite activities to do during this time of the year?
- What do you tend to wear during this season?
- What smells do you associate with this time of year?
- What is a good memory you have during this time of year?

Insight Into the Question

Hot and sunny, or cold and rainy? People's tastes differ. This question reveals what seasons and weather teens prefer.

Quick Additions

- What is your favorite kind of weather?
- Why do you like this weather?
- What is a good memory you have related to this weather?

Conversation SPRINGBOARD 135

What is one habit you wish you could break?

Follow-Up Questions

- Why do you want to break this habit?
- How would your life change?
- What is something you could do instead?

Insight Into the Question

This line of questioning gets kids thinking about their habits, both good and bad.

Quick Additions

- What are some good habits you have?
- Why are these good?
- What are some other good habits you'd like to have?
- What would your life be like with these habits?

Conversation SPRINGBOARD 136

When were you the most scared in your life? Why?

Follow-Up Questions

- How did you respond?
- How did the situation resolve?
- Could this situation happen again? Is there something you could do to avoid it?

Insight Into the Question

This question gives your child a chance to reflect on a memory of being scared and then examines fears in general.

Quick Additions

- What is the scariest movie you've seen?
- What do you do when you're scared?
- Who do you usually go to for comfort?

Conversation SPRINGBOARD 137

Fast-forward thirty years. What is the best compliment someone could give you about your children?

Follow-Up Questions

- Why would this be such a compliment?
- What would this be saying about you?
- Is there anything you can do in the next thirty years to make this a reality?

Insight Into the Question

This question gets kids thinking about parenting and how the choices they make now might affect how they parent later.

Quick Additions

- How many kids do you want to have?
- Boys, girls, both?
- How far apart do you want to have them?
- How old do you want to be when you have children?

- If you had to pick their names today, what would you name them?

Conversation SPRINGBOARD 138

What is the greatest physical pain you've ever experienced?

Follow-Up Questions

- How did it finally stop?
- Can you avoid that situation in the future? If so, how?
- Have you grown or learned anything from that experience?

Insight Into the Question

This question looks at pain and endurance, and hopefully how to overcome struggles.

Quick Additions

- What is the greatest feat or challenge you have endured?
- What is the most demanding exercise you have ever done (a one-hour run, three-hour hike, etc.)?
- How do you motivate yourself to keep going through tough times?

Conversation SPRINGBOARD 139

Batman and Spider-Man get into an all-out brawl. Who wins? Explain.

Follow-Up Questions

- What is your favorite superhero film?

- Who is your favorite superhero?
- If you could be one superhero, which would you want to be?

Insight Into the Question

This fun line of questioning taps in to teens' creative side, asking about superheroes and superpowers.

Quick Additions

- Who was the best villain ever, in TV, movies, or comics?
- What made this person such an effective bad guy?
- Which superhero would you want by your side if you had to battle this villain?
- How would you battle this villain?

Conversation SPRINGBOARD 140

Who do you wish you could get a compliment from, and why?

Follow-Up Questions

- What compliment do you wish they'd give you?
- Why would this compliment feel so good?
- Is there anyone else in your life who would give you a compliment like this?

Insight Into the Question

This question explores affirmation and the areas in our lives we hope people notice.

Quick Additions

- Name a compliment you have given someone recently.
- Who is someone you know who could really use some affirmation or a compliment?
- How could you affirm that person?
- When could you affirm them this week?

Conversation SPRINGBOARD 141

If you could speak another language, what would it be, and why?

Follow-Up Questions

- Where is the first place you'd use this language?
- What would you want to say?
- Where could you use this language the most in your future?
- How can you begin learning this language now?

Insight Into the Question

This question explores culture and education, particularly what languages our kids would enjoy knowing.

Quick Additions

- If you were a foreign exchange student for one year in another country, where would you want to go?
- Why this country?
- What would you want to do while you're there?
- Describe the family you'd like to stay with.

Conversation SPRINGBOARD 142

If you were forced to choose a different first name, which name would you want?

Follow-Up Questions

- Why this name?
- Do you know anyone with this name?
- What kind of person usually has this name?

Insight Into the Question

This creative question explores names and impressions we have about people.

Quick Additions

- What is the most interesting name you've come across?
- What name would you never want?
- What is the most creative dog name?
- What is the best dog name that a human could actually have?

Conversation SPRINGBOARD 143

What is your favorite social networking site, and why?

Follow-Up Questions

- How much time do you spend on this site each day?
- What is your favorite thing to do on this site?
- Who is the person you probably dialogue the most with on this site?

Insight Into the Question

This question gives you a peek into your teen's world of social media.

Quick Additions

- Describe the weirdest thing you've seen on this site.
- Describe the strangest person you ever talked with.
- Describe when you were the most hurt by someone on this site.

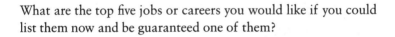

Conversation SPRINGBOARD 144

What are the top five jobs or careers you would like if you could list them now and be guaranteed one of them?

Follow-Up Questions

- Which of these five jobs would probably take the most time, and consequently, give you less time for yourself or your family?
- Which of these five jobs would probably give you the most time for yourself or your family?
- How much money do people in these jobs earn each year?
- How much does money influence your choice in a career?

Insight Into the Question

This question explores the jobs kids might want and the ramifications of choosing certain careers.

Quick Additions

- What job would you never ever want?

- What is it about this job that stinks?
- What might be a good aspect about this bad job?

Conversation SPRINGBOARD 145

What is your favorite snack or food that is uniquely found at places such as carnivals or state fairs?

Follow-Up Questions

- What is a good memory related to eating this food?
- Where would you have to drive today to get this food?
- When is the next time you can probably have this food?

Insight Into the Question

This question explores the connections between special foods and out-of-the-ordinary places.

Quick Additions

- What is your favorite snack at the mall?
- What is your favorite snack at the movie theater?
- What is your favorite snack for long car drives?

Conversation SPRINGBOARD 146

If school were canceled for one day tomorrow (for a teacher strike), what would you do?

Follow-Up Questions

- If you could have one friend with you, who would you invite?
- Why this person?
- If you could include a few more friends, who would you invite, and why?
- Which scenario would you enjoy the most: being alone, being with one friend, or a few? Why?

Insight Into the Question

This question is an imaginative way to learn more about your teen's friends and interests.

Quick Additions

- Describe your schedule for the day.
- How would your plans for the day change depending on how many friends were there?
- Want to plan a day like this on an upcoming Saturday?

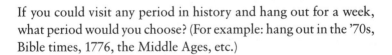

Conversation SPRINGBOARD 147

If you could visit any period in history and hang out for a week, what period would you choose? (For example: hang out in the '70s, Bible times, 1776, the Middle Ages, etc.)

Follow-Up Questions

- Why this time period?
- Is there anyone from this period you would hope to meet?
- What would you want to ask this person?

Insight Into the Question

This question can be nostalgic, historical, or just pure fantasy. But it stimulates imagination and helps us better understand some of their interests and opinions.

Quick Additions

- If you could take someone with you to this time period, who would you take?
- What would be your biggest fear visiting this time period?
- What are you thankful for now that didn't exist back then?
- Is there something that was better then, compared with now?

Conversation SPRINGBOARD 148

If you could ask God one question, what would you ask?

Follow-Up Questions

- How do you think he would answer?
- What do you hope he wouldn't say?
- Why do you want to know?

Insight Into the Question

This question explores teens' questions about God and perhaps reveals where their faith stands.

Quick Additions

- Describe God.
- Describe heaven.
- Who goes there?

Read the following passage:

And this is the testimony: God has given us eternal life, and this life is in his Son. Whoever has the Son has life; whoever does not have the Son of God does not have life. I write these things to you who believe in the name of the Son of God so that you may know that you have eternal life.

1 John 5:11–13

- According to these verses, what do you need to have life?
- What does it mean when someone "has the Son"?
- What does it look like these days when someone truly believes in Jesus, the Son of God?

Conversation SPRINGBOARD 149

If you got in huge trouble and needed someone to talk to, someone who would encourage you, who would you call?

Follow-Up Questions

- Why this person?
- What would he or she say to you?
- How has this person been a support to you in the past?

Insight Into the Question

This question gives you insight into who your teen trusts and feels safe talking to.

Quick Additions

- Is there someone who might choose you if they were asked the same question above?
- What kind of qualities would you need to demonstrate for someone to pick you?

GET YOUR TEENAGER TALKING

- What are some ways to demonstrate those qualities this week, month, and year?

Conversation SPRINGBOARD 150

If you could get a brand-new cell phone, which one would you choose, and why?

Follow-Up Questions

- What new or additional features would this new phone have?
- What is the first thing you would do with the phone?
- Do you know anyone with this phone? What do they like about it?

Insight Into the Question

This question gives you a glimpse into your child's digital world. Most young people today love their digital devices and want very specific features on them.

Quick Additions

- Describe the day you got your first cell phone.
- What was the first thing you did with it?
- Who did you first call or text?

Conversation SPRINGBOARD 151

If you could start a trend at your school, what would it be?

Follow-Up Questions

- Why this trend?
- How would your campus change?
- How important is it to you to make a positive change?
- If you had the opportunity, what kind of positive change would you like to make?

Insight Into the Question

This question gets young people thinking about the power they have to make an impact in their world.

Quick Additions

- Describe some trends you've noticed in the last few years.
- How did these trends affect your campus or community?
- How do you think these trends began?

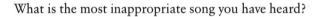

Conversation SPRINGBOARD 152

What is the most inappropriate song you have heard?

Follow-Up Questions

- What is the message of this song?
- Why is this song inappropriate?
- What message do you think people get from this song?
- Do you think they believe it? Explain.

Insight Into the Question

This question candidly asks kids about inappropriate music and then asks them to dissect its content. Enter this line of questioning cautiously and without judgment.

Quick Additions

- If people listen to several hours of this kind of music per day, do you think it would affect them?
- Does it affect you?
- Do you have any songs right now that you probably should get rid of?

Conversation SPRINGBOARD 153

What is one thing you wish people knew or understood about you, but you don't think they do?

Follow-Up Questions

- What could you do to help them understand?
- How would you hope people would respond?
- How would your world change?

Insight Into the Question

This question encourages kids to open up about real issues that they feel unheard about. Then it prompts them to think about listening to others and stepping into their shoes.

Quick Additions

- What efforts can you make to better listen and understand your friends or family?
- Who is someone you know who could really use a friend right now?
- How can you reach out to them?

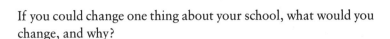

Conversation SPRINGBOARD 154

If you could change one thing about your school, what would you change, and why?

Follow-Up Questions

- What would this accomplish?
- How would school be different for you every day?
- Is this change possible? If so, how can you help make it happen?

Insight Into the Question

This question helps your child not only think about positive changes, but what they can do to catalyze change.

Quick Additions

- What do you like about your school that you wouldn't want changed?
- Which teachers or administrators do you hope won't leave anytime soon?
- What is it about these people that you like so much?

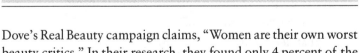

Conversation SPRINGBOARD 155

Dove's Real Beauty campaign claims, "Women are their own worst beauty critics." In their research, they found only 4 percent of the women in the world consider themselves beautiful. When women were asked to describe themselves, they all described themselves uglier than others described them.[18]

Why do you think so many woman think negatively about themselves?

145

Follow-Up Questions

- Which is more important, inner or outer beauty? Explain.
- Describe what makes someone beautiful and admirable inside.
- How long does inner beauty last? And outer beauty?
- What does Hollywood value more? Explain.

Insight Into the Question

This question probes into real beauty and self-esteem, particularly in females, and can lead to talks about external beauty compared to innermost character. (For a powerful video on the subject, search the Internet for "Dove's Real Beauty Sketches.")

Quick Additions

- How does someone develop their character—who they are inside?
- What are some of these internal qualities?

Read the following passage:

But the Lord said to Samuel, "Don't judge by his appearance or height, for I have rejected him. The Lord doesn't see things the way you see them. People judge by outward appearance, but the Lord looks at the heart."

1 Samuel 16:7 NLT

- How do people focus on outward appearances?
- How can this be misleading? Give an example.
- What does God focus on? Why?
- How can we allow God to change our hearts?

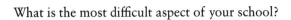

Conversation SPRINGBOARD 156

What is the most difficult aspect of your school?

Follow-Up Questions

- Why is this so difficult?
- How do you cope with it?
- Does this work?
- What would make this situation better (aside from completely escaping the situation)?

Insight Into the Question

This question deals with the realities of problem solving in difficult situations.

Quick Additions

- Who is someone you know who deals with difficult situations well?
- Describe ways they respond well.
- What can you learn from this person?

Conversation SPRINGBOARD 157

How much money do you think you should make each year to be happy?

Follow-Up Questions

- How did you come up with that number?
- Describe what your life would be like with this income.
- How much will income affect your happiness? Explain.

Insight Into the Question

This question gets teens thinking about the reality of salaries and living expenses.

Quick Additions

- If your boss offered you 10 percent more money to work 10 percent more hours per week, would you do it? Why or why not?
- When does work, even school work, start to interfere with your personal and family time?
- How can laziness interfere with making a good income?

Conversation SPRINGBOARD 158

What is the best way to deal with tragedy?

Follow-Up Questions

- How would this help?
- Name a tragedy you experienced and how you responded.
- How could you have responded better?
- What is a healthy response in this situation?

Insight Into the Question

Parents might want to use discretion before opening this line of questioning. It prompts teens to reflect on personal tragedy and might stir up emotions if they've recently suffered a great loss, such as the death of a loved one.

Quick Additions

- What are some unhealthy ways of dealing with tragedy?

- How would these methods backfire?
- How can you be a friend and help someone through tragedy?

Conversation SPRINGBOARD 159

Your top five movies of all time. Go!

Follow-Up Questions

- If you could only choose one favorite, which would it be?
- If you had to drop one from your list, which would go?
- What is your best memory watching one of these films?
- If you could watch all five films right now, who would you want to join you for this movie marathon?

Insight Into the Question

This question digs into your teenager's taste in movies.

Quick Additions

- What would your top five movies have been five years ago?
- What is one of the worst films you've ever seen?
- What is the raunchiest film you've ever seen?
- What film is coming soon that you'd love to see?

Conversation SPRINGBOARD 160

Who is the person you hate disappointing the most?

Follow-Up Questions

- Why do you hate disappointing him (or her) so much?
- When is the last time you disappointed him or her?
- Is he or she right to be disappointed? Explain.
- If you were he or she, would you have been disappointed in "you" in this situation?
- What advice would you have given "you" in this situation?

Insight Into the Question

This question explores who our teenagers care about and how our actions affect our relationship with this person.

Quick Additions

- What is something you do that impresses or inspires others?
- Describe a time you did something that made someone proud.
- What is something you could do this week that you know would make someone proud?

Conversation SPRINGBOARD 161

Dogs or cats? The whole planet will be rid of one of the species, and you are the one who decides. Which is it?

Follow-Up Questions

- Why would you choose this way?
- What past experiences influenced your decision?
- Will you miss the other species? Explain.

Insight Into the Question

This creative question is just fun, but it also stimulates thinking about choices and their repercussions.

Quick Additions

- What do you like or dislike about dogs?
- What do you like or dislike about cats?
- Is there another animal you'd rather have instead of a dog or cat? What?

Conversation SPRINGBOARD 162

What's worse, when someone lies to you or steals from you? Why?

Follow-Up Questions

- Describe a time someone lied to you.
- How did this make you feel?
- Describe a time someone stole from you or someone close to you.
- How did you want to respond?
- How did you respond?

Insight Into the Question

This line of questioning deals with our reactions to those who hurt us.

Quick Additions

- Describe a time you lied to someone.
- How did they respond?

- What would have been the perfect way they could have responded?
- In Luke 6:31, Jesus said those famous words: "Do to others as you would like them to do to you" (NLT). Does that include times when they're mean to us? Explain.
- How should we respond when people hurt us?

Conversation SPRINGBOARD 163

What bad thing happened to you that turned out for the best?

Follow-Up Questions

- How did you respond when it first happened?
- How long was it before the situation resulted in some good?
- How did you respond then?
- What did you learn from the situation?

Insight Into the Question

This question gets teenagers thinking about how good can come out of bad situations.

Quick Additions

- Why do difficult situations often stretch us and cause us to grow?
- What character traits can be developed from tough situations?
- Who is someone you can go to in tough times?

Conversation SPRINGBOARD 164
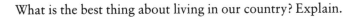

What is the best thing about living in our country? Explain.

Follow-Up Questions

- What is the worst?
- If you could live in any other country, where would you want to live? Why there?
- What is the biggest improvement needed in our country?
- How would life be different if that changed?

Insight Into the Question

This question prompts kids to think patriotically, and sheds perspective on what they like about our country.

Quick Additions

- If you had to live in another country, which one would you choose?
- How would life be different for you?
- Where would you not want to live?

Conversation SPRINGBOARD 165

Would your friends describe you the same as we (your parents) describe you? Why or why not?

Follow-Up Questions

- What would the biggest difference be in their descriptions of you?

- What would we and your friends both definitely include in our descriptions?
- Which is the real you? Explain.

Insight Into the Question

This question prompts teenagers to explore their actions in different company and venues.

Quick Additions

- Who can you completely relax around and just totally be yourself?
- What is it about this person that allows you to be this way?
- Who do you wish you could be this way with?

Conversation **SPRINGBOARD 166**

What would you say to a bully who was picking on someone you know?

Follow-Up Questions

- Would it work?
- What would work?
- Why do bullies bully?

Insight Into the Question

This question dives into the issue of bullying and helps your kids think of possible solutions.

Quick Additions

- Describe a time you felt bullied.

- Describe a time that someone might have described your actions as bullying.

Read the following passage:

Do nothing out of selfish ambition or vain conceit. Rather, in humility value others above yourselves, not looking to your own interests but each of you to the interests of the others.

Philippians 2:3–4

- How do these verses say we should value others?
- Give an example of valuing someone else above yourself.
- What do these verses say we should do rather than looking to our own interests?
- How can we look to the interests of others?
- What is one way you can live out the message of this passage this week?

Conversation SPRINGBOARD 167

Which job is tougher: magician or comedian? Why?

Follow-Up Questions

- What would be the best part about being a magician?
- What is the worst part?
- What is the best part about being a comedian?
- What is the worst part?
- If you had to do one of these two jobs, which would you want to do, and why?

Insight Into the Question

This "would you rather" question gives you a glimpse into your teenager's personal taste in vocations.

Quick Additions

- If you could be a successful entertainer of any kind, what would you be?
- Where would you live?
- What would your life be like?
- Could this be a reality? If so, what do you have to do this week (and month and year) to pursue this?

Conversation SPRINGBOARD 168

If you could see video footage of the earth's beginning or its end, which would you choose to watch? Why?

Follow-Up Questions

- What do you think you'd see?
- What do you hope you'd see?
- What do you hope not to see?

Insight Into the Question

This question prompts kids to think about the earth's beginning and possible end. This kind of conversation often makes people think about the bigger questions in life and what really matters.

Quick Additions

- If you knew the world was ending tomorrow, what would you do today?
- Who would you want to be with when the world ends?
- What happens then?

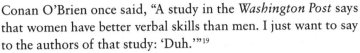

Conversation SPRINGBOARD 169

Conan O'Brien once said, "A study in the *Washington Post* says that women have better verbal skills than men. I just want to say to the authors of that study: 'Duh.'"[19]

Conan's comment is funny. But do you think there is truth to this study?

Follow-Up Questions

- Do you think women have better verbal skills? Why, or why not?
- In what ways are women often more skilled than men?
- In what ways are men often more skilled than women?
- Is this a bad thing? Explain.

Insight Into the Question

This question gets young people thinking about the different talents and abilities of each gender. It also could reveal stereotypes.

Quick Additions

- When you get married, what skill do you really hope your spouse has?
- What skill do you think your spouse will really hope you have?
- What would your marriage be like if you and your spouse had opposite skills? Would this be a bad thing? Explain.

Conversation SPRINGBOARD 170

If you could instantly memorize one book of the Bible, which book would you choose, and why?

Follow-Up Questions

- What are some elements you really like from this book?
- How could knowing these truths verbatim affect your daily life?
- How long would it take for someone to memorize this entire book? Is it even possible?
- Is that something you'd like to try (maybe in part)?

Insight Into the Question

This question urges young people to think about parts of the Bible that resonate with them. It also encourages them to consider memorizing sections of Scripture.

Quick Additions

- Can you recite a Bible verse right now?
- If so, what does that verse mean?
- How can that verse help someone you know?
- What passage of Scripture or Bible story could help your friends?

Conversation SPRINGBOARD 171

If you wanted (or had to get) a tattoo, what would you want, and where would it go on your body?

Follow-Up Questions

- What is the worst tattoo you've ever seen?
- What popular tattoo would you never want?
- If you found out that your future spouse had a tattoo, what would you want, and where on his (or her) body?

- What tattoo would you really hope your spouse doesn't have?

Insight Into the Question

This question gives you a little glimpse into teens' opinions about the growing fad of inking.

Quick Additions

- If Grandma wanted to get a tattoo, what would you advise her?
- If Mom (or Dad) wanted to get a tattoo, what would you advise her (or him)?
- Should a person use a novice tattoo artist to try to save money? Why or why not?

Conversation SPRINGBOARD 172

What sermon do you wish your pastor would preach? Explain.

Follow-Up Questions

- What would this accomplish?
- Why do you need to hear this message?
- How could this message change your life?
- Do you need to wait for the sermon? In other words, is there someone you can go to and receive this wisdom?

Insight Into the Question

This question gives you a peek into your teenager's perception of her own spiritual needs.

Quick Additions

- What is the best sermon you've ever heard?
- Why was it so good?
- How did it affect you?
- Do you need to hear it again? Explain.

Conversation SPRINGBOARD 173

If you could have one language implanted into your brain so you could instantly speak it fluently, which language would you choose, and why?

Follow-Up Questions

- Where is the first place you'd use this language?
- How would it make a difference in your life?
- Because it's impossible to plant languages in our brains and "instantly" speak, is it worth spending a few years learning a language? Explain.

Insight Into the Question

This fun question gets young people thinking about different cultures and languages.

Quick Additions

- What language will you probably take in school (or are you taking)?
- Why this language?
- Where will you use this?

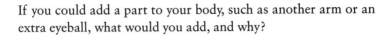

Conversation SPRINGBOARD 174

If you could add a part to your body, such as another arm or an extra eyeball, what would you add, and why?

Follow-Up Questions

- What is the first thing you'd do with this new body part?
- How would your life change?
- What drawbacks might arise?

Insight Into the Question

This creative question explores teenagers' imaginations and urges them to think through choices and consequences.

Quick Additions

- What body part do you use the least?
- What would life be like without it?
- What body part do you use the most?
- What would life be like without it?

Conversation SPRINGBOARD 175

What animal would you never eat if offered to you, and why?

Follow-Up Questions

- What is the most bizarre food you've eaten?
- What is the worst tasting dish you've had?
- What is the tastiest food you've eaten?

Insight Into the Question

This creative question simply explores our kids' tastes in bizarre foods.

Quick Additions

- What is the worst vegetable you've eaten?
- What is the yummiest fruit you've had?
- What is something you ate in the wild (fruit off of a tree, berries off of a bush, etc.)?

Conversation SPRINGBOARD 176

If you could make a permanent change to your hair—making it more thick, or thinner, curlier, straighter, darker, blonder, etc.—what would you choose, and why?

Follow-Up Questions

- How would your life change?
- Do you think you'd ever miss your old hair? Explain.
- Do you think others would support your hairstyle change?
- What is something positive about your hair right now?

Insight Into the Question

This discussion helps teenagers think about their own body image, allowing them to dream a little, but urging them to be thankful for who they are.

Quick Additions

- What is something you like about your looks and wouldn't want to change?

- What is something that someone else might like about your looks?
- What is something you like about who you are inside?
- What is something your friends like about who you are inside?

Conversation SPRINGBOARD 177

What product would you like to be the spokesperson for (Nike, Doritos, Huggies, etc.)?

Follow-Up Questions

- Why this product?
- How would your life change?
- If you were given an endless supply of this product, and just had to fill out an order form, what would you order for your first shipment?

Insight Into the Question

This fun question gives you a peek into your teenager's taste in brands.

Quick Additions

- What is a product you wouldn't mind representing, but you'd be afraid of what others think?
- What is a product you would definitely turn down if they offered you a deal to be their spokesperson? Explain.

Conversation SPRINGBOARD 178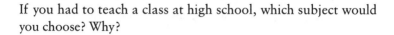

If you had to teach a class at high school, which subject would you choose? Why?

Follow-Up Questions

- What would you do differently than existing teachers?
- How would you hope kids would respond?
- Which subject would be the last class you'd ever want to teach? Why?

Insight Into the Question

This question prompts your kids to think creatively and reveals a little about the subjects they enjoy at school.

Quick Additions

- What age group would you enjoy teaching? Why?
- What age group would you not enjoy? Why?
- Is there a certain school you'd like to teach at? Which one? Why?

Conversation SPRINGBOARD 179

What is one thing you'd change about us (your parents), and why?

Follow-Up Questions

- Would this change be better or worse for you in the long run? Explain.
- Would this change be better for us? Explain.
- How would your life change?

Insight Into the Question

Only ask this question if you're prepared to hear the answer without overreacting. We can learn a lot from our kids' perceptions, even if they aren't totally logical or based on fact. Use this line of questioning to safely and tenderly explore how your relationship might improve with your teenager.

Quick Additions

- What is one thing you think we (your parents) might wish you'd change about yourself?
- Would this help you?
- Would you listen?

Conversation SPRINGBOARD 180

Mark Twain once said, "Anger is an acid that can do more harm to the vessel in which it is stored than to anything on which it is poured."
Explain what you think he meant by this.

Follow-Up Questions

- Is Twain right about anger?
- Give an example of what this might look like, hypothetically.
- When have you seen this in real life?

Insight Into the Question

This question explores the consequences of anger and bitterness.

Quick Additions

- When is anger a good thing?

- When does anger become a bad thing?
- What do you call it when someone stores anger, and it festers and boils into something else? (Possible answers: bitterness, resentment, passive-aggressive behaviors.)
- How do you keep anger from turning into something unhealthy such as bitterness or resentment?

Acknowledgments

Much love to my family for their patience with me when I slipped away to the patio to write each day. Thanks especially for the times they joined me out there, sitting with me, watching the cats pretend they're lions in the back lawn.

Thanks to my girls, Alyssa and Ashley, for coming up with some of these questions with me. Your creativity is amazing and your honesty helps keep me relevant!

Thanks to friends for helping me with other questions. I especially thank my friend David R. Smith. You have such a servant's heart. And thanks to Andy Matzke for humoring me when I told him he couldn't leave the table until he gave me ten questions. He gave me some good ones!

Thanks to all my blog readers at JonathanMcKeeWrites.com for all your good ideas. I've gleaned many good questions and ideas from your comments on my blog. Thanks for being loyal readers!

Most of all, thanks to Jesus for being such a good model of asking good questions where so many others would have lectured.

Notes

1. Cathy Payne, "Minding Your P's and Q's When Texting," *USA Today*, February 11, 2013, http://www.usatoday.com/story/news/nation/2013/02/08/mobile-device-etiquette/1894737/.

2. "Sex Book Filled With 200 Blank Pages Storms Up Charts," *Metro*, March 3, 2011, http://metro.co.uk/2011/03/03/sex-book-filled-with-200-blank-pages-storms-up-charts-642205/.

3. "Freshman Women's Binge Drinking Tied to Sexual Assault Risk," *Journal of Studies on Alcohol and Drugs*, January 2012 press release, http://alcoholstudies.rutgers.edu/news/JSADpress/JSADJan2012.pdf.

4. Janelle Nanos, "Millennials Love Gadgets More Than They Love Cars," *Boston Daily*, February 28, 2013, http://www.bostonmagazine.com/news/blog/2013/02/28/millennials-love-their-computers-more-than-cars/.

5. Joseph Berger, "Some Wonder if Cash for Good Test Scores Is the Wrong Kind of Lesson," *New York Times*, August 8, 2007, http://www.nytimes.com/2007/08/08/education/08education.html.

6. Survey results from The Barna Group, reported by Jim Hinch, "Hinch: Youth Increasingly Seeking New Salvation," *Orange County Register*, August 21, 2013, http://www.ocregister.com/articles/church-380418-young-people.html.

7. "Infographic: Unprepared for College," http://www.usatodayeducate.com/staging/index.php/infographic-unprepared-for-college.

8. "Movies Influence Teen Alcohol Consumption More Than Parents, Study Finds," NewsCore, February 21, 2012, http://www.foxnews.com/health/2012/02/21/movies-influence-teen-alcohol-consumption-more-than-parents-study-finds/.

9. Survey results from Laura Hamilton, University of California–Merced, originally published in the *American Sociological Review*, as reported by Scott Jaschik, "Spoiled Children," *Inside Higher Ed*, January 14, 2013, http://www.insidehighered.com/news/2013/01/14/study-finds-increased-parental-support-college-results-lower-grades.

10. Barna Group, "Athletes Influence Greater Than Faith Leaders," February 2, 2013, https://www.barna.org/component/content/article/36-homepage-main-promo/602-barna-update-01-23-2013.

11. Rick Nauert, "Teen Health Linked to Teen Happiness," PsychCentral.com, March 5, 2012, http://psychcentral.com/news/2012/03/05/teen-health-linked-to-teen-happiness/35578.html.

12. Larry Copeland, "Texting in Traffic: Adults Worse Than Teens," *USA Today,* March 28, 2013, http://www.usatoday.com/story/news/nation/2013/03/28/adults-worse-than-teens-about-texting-behind-wheel/2026331/.

13. Shannon Proudfoot, "Over 1 in 4 Teens and Young Adults Addicted to Tanning: Study," Canwest News Service, http://www.canada.com/health/Over+teens+young+adults+addicted+tanning+Study/797099/story.html.

14. "Tennessee Hopes Shame Will Help Combat Drunk Driving," Associated Press/FoxNews.com, December 31, 2005, http://www.foxnews.com/story/2005/12/31/tennessee-hopes-shame-will-help-combat-drunk-driving/.

15. Martin Luther King Jr., *Strength to Love* (New York: HarperCollins, 1977), 53.

16. Investigators used a national sample of 26,069 adolescents aged 11 to 15 years who participated in the 2010 Canadian Health Behavior in School-Aged Children study. Results reported by Rick Nauert, "Family Dinners Can Bolster Teens' Mental Health," PsychCentral.com, http://psychcentral.com/news/2013/03/21/family-dinners-can-bolster-teens-mental-health/52849.html.

17. Albert Camus, *The Minotaur.* Essay found at http://www.sccs.swarthmore.edu/users/00/pwillen1/lit/minot.htm.

18. Dove's Real Beauty Campaign, http://www.youtube.com/user/doveunitedstates.

19. Conan O'Brien, http://www.brainyquote.com/quotes/authors/c/conan_obrien.html.

Index

Note: Numbers are Conversation Springboard numbers (not page numbers)

Note: Numbers are Conversation Springboard numbers (not page numbers)

Jonathan McKee is an expert on youth culture and the author of more than a dozen books, including *The Guy's Guide to God, Girls, and the Phone in Your Pocket* and *The Zombie Apocalypse Survival Guide for Teenagers*. He has twenty years of youth-ministry experience and speaks to parents and leaders worldwide. He also writes about parenting and youth culture while providing free resources at TheSource4Parents.com. Jonathan, his wife, Lori, and their three kids live in California. Learn more at JonathanMcKeeWrites.com and Twitter.com/InJonathansHead.